Presented to

My loving husband

on the occasion of

Our First Anniversary

from

Your loving wife

This book entitles you to pick one
recipe per month that I will cook -- no
questions asked!

Love,

Ann

Cooking By The Bootstraps

A Taste Of Oklahoma Heaven
Cooked Up By
The Junior Welfare League Of
Enid, Oklahoma

Copyright © 2002
Junior Welfare League of Enid
201 W. Owen K. Garriott
Enid, Oklahoma 73701
580-234-2665

ISBN: 0-9609340-1-4

Designed, Edited, and Manufactured by
Favorite Recipes® Press
An imprint of

FRP™

P.O. Box 305142
Nashville, Tennessee 37230
1-800-358-0560

Art Director: Steve Newman
Designer: David Malone
Project Manager: Susan Larson
Editor: Debbie Van Mol

Manufactured in the United States of America
First Printing: 2002   15,000 copies

Tried and true, not necessarily new, recipes and memories from
The Junior Welfare League of Enid, Oklahoma.
Improved, improvised, and perfected over the years.

Table of Contents

*The Junior Welfare League
of Enid, Oklahoma
is an organization of women
committed to improving our community
through volunteerism and generosity.*

* * * * * * * * * * * * * *

As we begin our 71st year,
we can look back
at the ingredients to our success.
A group of women committed
to giving of their time and talent
to help those in need.
A recipe passed down from
generation to generation.
Each generation adding
their own special flavor.

Annie Dillingham, President 2000–2001

4

Preface

The cuisine of Oklahoma is as rich and diverse as its people. Our multi-cultural heritage comes from generations of people who have weathered bad times, and cherished the good. During lean years, Oklahoma's grandmothers prepared wonderful meals from meager ingredients. A plentiful harvest meant even better things.

Over the years, Oklahoma produced many unique things. From the independent oilmen to the century farm, family names continue to mold our community. The cooks of today's Oklahoma continue in this rich tradition.

The following pages reflect the taste of Oklahoma; past, present, and future. I mention the future, because no matter the adversity, Oklahomans persevere. From the dust bowl days to the boom time, Oklahomans embrace it all. Tornadoes, floods, storms, and drought. They rally, regroup, and begin again. Hardscrabble, true-grit, and salt-of-the-earth were all terms invented for Okies. They pick themselves up BY THE BOOTSTRAPS, and go on.

So put on your apron and meet me in the kitchen. It's time to cook up a little slice of Oklahoma heaven.

Gabriella Wilson, Cookbook Publishing Chair

Our very special thanks to Jim Nay for photographing our front and back cover, as well as all the chapter title photos. Jim has operated a full-service photography studio in Enid, Oklahoma, since 1965. He specializes in portraiture, editorial, and all types of commercial photography. In Enid, Jim is considered the "master of black and white photography." His photographs have won international acclaim and many professional awards. However, Jim is most proud that his photographs "win a place in the heart."

Patrons

GOLDEN APRON PATRONS
Peter and Annie Dillingham
Henson Construction
Ann Frazee Riley
Elbert and Meme Wheeler

SILVER SPOON PATRONS
Dr. G. Franklin and Judy Forney
Randy and Lori Long

BRONZE BOWL PATRONS
Gretchen and Alan Boyer
Charlie and Kelli Cannon
Robert and Sandra Emery
Chris and Lori Markes
Bud and Jo Ann Nicholas
Shannon L. Waken, CPA

"COOKING BY THE BOOTSTRAPS" ADVERTISERS
Boys Market
Enid Pet Hospital
Ward Petroleum Corporation
Greenbrier Village
EnidHomes.com

And special thanks to Nottingham Collection Antiques, Mini Mall Antiques, Corral West Ranchwear, Jumbo Foods, Winter Livestock, Mashell Swenn, *Enid News and Eagle,* and Cindy Choate.

Committees

Gabriella Wilson, *Publishing Chair*
Tracy Shimanek, *Co-Chair*
Anna Irwin, *Co-Chair*

Katy Atwood, *Recipe Testing Chair*
Kelli Cannon, *Co-Chair*

Toni Yancer, *Recipe Tasting Coordinator*
Traci Straw, *Co-Chair*
Katrena Winter, *Co-Chair*

Judy Stevison, *Marketing*
Shannon Waken, *Finance*

CHAPTER COMMITTEES

APPETIZERS & BEVERAGES
Shaye Sheppard, *Chair*
Heidi Cameron, *Co-Chair*
Christi Holland
Raymie Holland
Kristy Pendleton
Cathy Rose
Ann Schmitt
Sharla Zuech

SALADS, SEAFOOD & PASTA
Annette Burgart, *Chair*
Lori Shearer, *Co-Chair*
Becky Crawford
April Davis
Pam Gale
Marie-Jean Lopez
Mary Merrit
Teryl Snodgrass

BREAKFAST, BREADS & VEGGIES
Amy Johnson, *Chair*
Cheryl Martens, *Co-Chair*
Teresa Benway
Mary Clare-Moser
Holly Hamm-Boyd
Jennifer Harmon
Karey Henderson
Jill Phillips
Molly Player
Linda Yauk

SOUPS, STEWS & SAUCES
Linda Outhier, *Chair*
Mary Armstrong, *Co-Chair*
Paula Benge
Shelly Coulter
Mika Dick
Mary Fischaber
Traci Hendrix
Nancy Jeronimus
Lynette Luttrell

MAIN DISHES
Tricia Keeler-Felt, *Chair*
Bengi Beebe, *Co-Chair*
Kim Barnthouse
Jean Bergstrom
Jill Holthoff
Kim Milacek
Melann Reid
Faith Sarver
Cicily Staerkel
Darci Winter
Sherry Wolff

SWEETS
Renee Winklejohn, *Chair*
Shelly White, *Co-Chair*
Melissa Atkinson
Kathy Burge
Cindy Choate
Lora Jacks
Lori Morrison
Kristin Sucich
Denise Tucker

ALL RECIPES WERE PREPARED AND TASTED BY JWL MEMBERS, INCLUDING: Kelly Anderson, Kelly Callant, Patricia Chesshir, Michelle Dick, Annie Dillingham, Lisa Dillingham, Melody Manahan, Jill McCarley, Tracy Nicholas, Nelda Ream, Pam Schoenhals, Deb Sexton, Bonnie Shaw, and Leslie Weldon.

Beyond Salt and Pepper

Spice market in Provence, France. Photo by Mimi Rippee

Do you want to add a taste of Italy to a favorite dish but aren't confident about Italian ingredients? Are you intrigued by Indian cuisine but aren't familiar with the seasonings? Want to have a summer party and provide a Caribbean flair to your buffet?

Now you can do all of these and more with this easy-to-use chart designed by Mimi Rippee. She teaches with charts like this one to show how easy it is to turn a simple dish into one internationally inspired, simply with the addition of significant ingredients and seasonings.

For example, if you want a salad to complement a Mexican meal, add jicama, carrot, and avocado. For the dressing, add cumin to a lemon juice dressing. And olé!

Want the salad to scream, "I'm in southern France?" Add fresh shallots and Dijon mustard to a white wine vinaigrette. To the salad, add tomatoes and blanched beans, then a few Niçoise olives. Voila!

How about a salad that incorporates tropical flavors? Add black beans, then sprinkle the salad with goat cheese. Blend a piece of fresh mango into your basic vinaigrette and you're ready to reggae!

It's that easy! There are no rules. Use what you have and use what you like! But go beyond salt and pepper!

	MEXICAN	ITALIAN	GREEK	FRENCH
HERBS	Oregano, cilantro, parsley, bay leaf, mint	Oregano, basil, rosemary, fennel, sage, thyme, flat-leafed parsley, marjoram	Mint, oregano, marjoram, bay leaf, parsley, dill, rosemary	Parsley, bay leaf, thyme, savory, sage, basil, mint, rosemary, tarragon, herbes de Provence
SPICES	Coriander, cumin, cinnamon, ground chile pepper, anise, allspice, clove	Cayenne pepper	Cinnamon, cloves, juniper berries	White pepper, juniper berries, anise, allspice, cinnamon, clove, quatre epices
OTHER SEASONINGS	Onion, garlic, mole, adobo, fresh and dried chile peppers, salsa, pico de gallo, vanilla	Onion, garlic, scallions, pesto	Onion, garlic	Onion, garlic, shallot, chives, scallions, Dijon mustard, vanilla
VEGETABLES	Tomato, tomatillo, jicama, avocado, carrot, corn, squash	Tomato, mushroom, arugula, radicchio, eggplant, spinach, zucchini, peas	Tomato, cucumber, eggplant, spinach	Leek, mushroom, endive, cabbage, tomato, green bean, eggplant, beet, celery root, potato, white asparagus, zucchini, carrot
FRUITS	Lime, lemon, orange, plantain, guava, mango	Lemon, orange, fig, prune, grapes, apple, raisins, citron	Lemon, dates, grapes, currants	Berries, apple, prunes, plums, cherries, fig, pear, currant, citron, lemon
NUTS/SEEDS	Pumpkin seeds, pine nuts, almonds, pecans, sesame seeds	Pine nuts, hazelnuts, almonds, pistachios	Walnuts, almonds, pine nuts	Almonds, walnuts, pistachios, hazelnuts, chestnuts
CHEESE/DAIRY	Queso fresco, cream, cajeta	Mozzarella, Parmesan, Gorgonzola, goat cheese, mascarpone, ricotta, cream	Kefalotiri, feta cheese, yogurt	Gruyère, chèvre, butter, Parmesan, cream, crème fraiche
LIQUIDS	Vinegar	Wine (vinsanto, grappa, marsala, barolo), olive oil, vinegar (red wine, balsamic), espresso	Red wine vinegar, olive oil, ouzo	Red and white wine, vinegar (red wine, white wine, Champagne), port, Champagne, Cognac, Calvados, olive oil
MISCELLANEOUS	Green olives, chorizo, pinto beans, chick-peas, rice, tortillas (flour and corn), Mexican chocolate	Olives, prosciutto, pancetta, capers, anchovies, arborio rice, honey, pasta, polenta, chick-peas, truffles, white beans	Kalamata olives, honey, phyllo pastry, orzo, grape leaves, capers	Niçoise olives, truffles, anchovies, capers, salt pork, foie gras, caviar, lentils, white beans, chocolate

A self-proclaimed *bon vivant*, Mimi Rippee works as a personal chef, caterer, recipe developer, and food writer. "I love everything about food—shopping for it, cooking it, reading and writing about it, and, of course, eating it!" Inspired by her French mother's passion for international cuisines, Mimi's culinary quest is to continue experimenting, whether in her own kitchen or when traveling. As Mimi puts it, "So much food, so little time!"

This chart is not meant to be a complete listing of ingredients. In fact, it is extremely difficult to generalize a cuisine when many culinary regions exist in a country. I have listed the most significant as well as readily available ingredients, most of which can be purchased at supermarkets.

INDIAN	LATIN AMERICAN/CARIBBEAN	CHINESE	MIDDLE EASTERN	
Saffron, cilantro, mint, parsley, basil, bay leaf	Cilantro, oregano, parsley, thyme, marjoram	Cilantro	Dill, saffron, parsley, mint	HERBS
Cumin, coriander, turmeric, cinnamon, mustard, clove, cardamom, paprika, fennel, nutmeg, fenugreek, cayenne pepper	Cayenne pepper, nutmeg, allspice, annatto, anise, coriander, clove, cumin, cinnamon, paprika	5-spice powder, Szchewan peppercorns, star anise	Paprika, cayenne pepper, cinnamon, allspice, cumin, cardamom, nutmeg, coriander, turmeric	SPICES
Onion, garlic, ginger, chutney, hot chile paste, garam masala (curry powder), fresh chile peppers	Onion, garlic, jerk, Tabasco sauce, Pickapeppa Sauce, mole, fresh and dried chile peppers, chipotle	Onion, garlic, ginger, green onions, hoisin sauce, chile pepper paste, fermented black beans, oyster sauce, red bean paste, dried chile peppers	Onion, garlic, ginger, harissa, tahini	OTHER SEASONINGS
Peas, spinach, potato, cauliflower, cucumber	Corn, sweet potato, avocado, tomato, potato, pumpkin, hominy	Onion, garlic, green onions, green pepper, mushroom, bok choy, bean sprouts, snow peas, tomato, cucumber	Onion, garlic, tomato, cucumber, ginger, eggplant, spinach, potato	VEGETABLES
Coconut, guava, lemon, lime, mango, raisins	Plantain, mango, coconut, orange, lemon, lime	Lychee nuts, wintermelon, kumquats, mandarin orange	Lemon, pomegranate, apricot, raisins, dates, currants, orange	FRUITS
Almonds, pistachios, sesame seeds, white poppy seeds, black mustard seeds, cashews, caraway seeds	Pumpkin seeds, almonds, walnuts, pecans	Pine nuts, cashews, peanuts, almonds, white and black sesame seeds	Sesame seeds, walnuts, almonds, pine nuts, poppy seeds	NUTS/SEEDS
Yogurt, panir (homemade cheese), cream ghee (clarified butter)	Cream, queso blanco		Yogurt, goat cheese	CHEESE/DAIRY
	Vinegar, muscatel, tequila, annatto oil	Rice wine vinegar, peanut oil, chile oil, sesame oil, soy sauce	Olive oil, red wine vinegar, ouzo	LIQUIDS
Dal (legumes), basmati rice, chick-pea flour	Black beans, flour and corn tortillas, rice, chorizo, masa harina, Mexican chocolate	Bamboo shoots, water chestnuts, dried mushrooms, rice, bean curd, cellophane noodles, Chinese sausage	Olives, fava beans, lentils, rice, chick-peas, bulgur, grape leaves	MISCELLANEOUS

Appetizers & Beverages

Chunky Artichoke Salsa with Pita Chips

1 (6-ounce) jar marinated
   artichoke hearts,
   drained, chopped
5 Roma tomatoes, coarsely
   chopped

1/4 cup chopped black
   olives
2 tablespoons chopped
   red onion
1 garlic clove, crushed

2 tablespoons minced
   fresh basil
Salt and pepper to taste
4 pita bread rounds

Combine the artichokes, tomatoes, olives, onion, garlic and basil in a bowl and mix gently. Season with salt and pepper. Serve immediately or let stand at room temperature for 1 hour to enhance the flavor.

Split the pita rounds into halves. Cut each round into 8 wedges. Arrange the wedges in a single layer on a baking stone. Spray the wedges lightly with nonstick olive oil baking spray. Bake for 8 to 10 minutes or until crisp; watch closely to prevent overbrowning. Serve with the salsa.

Makes 2 cups salsa and 64 chips

* * * * * * * * * * * * * * * * * * * *

Aspen Salsa

1 (16-ounce) jar taco sauce
2 (10-ounce) cans diced
   tomatoes with green chiles
2 bunches green onions,
   chopped

1 to 2 (4-ounce) cans
   chopped black olives,
   drained
2 tomatoes, chopped
1 tablespoon lemon juice

2 tablespoons Cavender's
   Greek seasoning
1 teaspoon garlic powder
Tortilla chips

Combine the taco sauce, undrained tomatoes, green onions, olives, tomatoes, lemon juice, Cavender's Greek seasoning and garlic powder in a bowl and mix well. Serve with tortilla chips or other dippers.

Serves 8 to 10

Black Bean Salsa

1 (15-ounce) can black
   beans, drained, rinsed
1 (10-ounce) can diced
   tomatoes with green
   chiles
1 cup chopped tomato

1/2 cup chopped fresh
   cilantro
1/4 cup red wine vinegar
1 bunch green onions,
   chopped
3 tablespoons lime juice

1 garlic clove, minced
1/4 teaspoon cumin
1/8 teaspoon cayenne
   pepper
Chili powder to taste
Tortilla chips

Combine the beans, undrained tomatoes, tomato, cilantro, wine vinegar, green onions, lime juice, garlic, cumin, cayenne pepper and chili powder in a bowl and mix well. Chill, covered, until serving time. Serve with tortilla chips.

   Serves 8 to 10

* *

Corn Salsa

2 (16-ounce) cans whole
   kernel corn, drained
4 Roma tomatoes, chopped
4 small avocados, chopped
1 (4-ounce) can diced green
   chiles, drained

1 (4-ounce) can sliced black
   olives, drained
1 bunch green onions,
   chopped
2 to 4 tablespoons chopped
   fresh cilantro

1/8 teaspoon garlic salt
1 (8-ounce) bottle Italian
   salad dressing
Tortilla chips

Combine the corn, tomatoes, avocados, green chiles, olives, green onions, cilantro and garlic salt in a bowl and mix gently. Add the salad dressing and toss to coat. Chill, covered, for 8 to 10 hours. Serve with tortilla chips.

   Serves 15

Mango Salsa

2 cups chopped fresh or
  canned mangoes
  (fresh is best)
1 cup chopped tomato
1/2 cup chopped fresh
  cilantro

1/4 cup chopped purple
  onion
2 fresh serrano chiles,
  chopped
1 garlic clove, minced
1/4 cup fresh lime juice

1 tablespoon olive oil
1 tablespoon red wine
  vinegar
1/2 teaspoon hot sauce
1/2 teaspoon cumin
1/4 teaspoon pepper

Combine the mangoes, tomato, cilantro, onion, serrano chiles and garlic in a bowl and mix gently. Add the lime juice, olive oil, wine vinegar, hot sauce, cumin and pepper and toss to coat. Chill, covered, for 4 to 10 hours. Serve with tortilla chips or as an accompaniment to beef, fish or poultry.

Serves 12 to 15

✳ ✳

Bread Pot Fondue

1 (8- to 10-inch) round loaf
  bread, such as Hawaiian
  bread
2 cups shredded sharp
  Cheddar cheese
1 1/2 cups sour cream

6 ounces cream cheese,
  softened
1 cup chopped cooked ham
  or dried beef
1 (4-ounce) can chopped
  green chiles, drained

1/2 cup chopped green
  onions
1 teaspoon Worcestershire
  sauce
2 tablespoons vegetable oil
1 tablespoon butter, melted

Slice off the top of the bread and reserve. Remove the center carefully, leaving a 1/2-inch shell. Cut the bread from the center into 1-inch cubes.

Combine the Cheddar cheese, sour cream and cream cheese in a mixing bowl and beat until blended. Stir in the ham, green chiles, green onions and Worcestershire sauce. Spoon into the bread shell. Replace the reserved top. Wrap the loaf in several layers of foil and place on a baking sheet. Bake at 350 degrees for 70 minutes or until heated through.

Combine the oil and butter in a bowl and mix well. Add the bread cubes and toss to coat. Arrange the bread cubes in a single layer on a baking sheet. Toast at 350 degrees for 10 minutes or until light brown. Serve the dip with the toasted bread cubes, fresh vegetables and/or assorted party crackers.

Serves 12 to 15

Melted Brie in Crust

2 round loaves sourdough
  bread

$1/2$ cup olive oil or butter
5 garlic cloves, minced

1 ($1^1/2$-pound) round Brie
  cheese

Cut the top from 1 of the bread loaves and discard. Remove the center carefully, leaving a $1/2$-inch shell. Make cuts $1^1/2$ inches apart and $1^1/2$ inches deep around the rim of the loaf. Cut the bread from the center and from the remaining loaf into $1/2$-inch cubes.

Combine the olive oil and garlic in a bowl and mix well. Brush the inside of the bread shell and bread cubes with the olive oil mixture. Remove the rind from the Brie if desired. Fit the Brie in the bread shell.

Place the filled bread shell on a baking sheet with sides. Arrange the bread cubes around the shell. Bake at 350 degrees for 10 minutes. Remove the bread cubes to a platter. Bake the filled shell for 10 minutes longer or until the cheese is melted and bubbly. Remove the bread shell to a serving platter. Serve with the toasted bread cubes.

Serves 30

The run into the Cherokee Outlet was one of the most dramatic events of the nineteenth century. When the lines broke just before the noon signal on September 16, 1893, the wildest land grab in recorded history was on in earnest.

In a single hour, over one hundred thousand had entered the Cherokee Outlet. Before the day was out, there was a family on nearly every quarter section in the territory.

That night across what had once been barren prairie, thousands of campfires twinkled. Enid had burst into being in a single day. Within a week, Enid had a population of over ten thousand.

Spinach and Artichoke Bake

1 (10-ounce) package frozen chopped spinach, thawed, drained

8 ounces cream cheese or reduced-fat cream cheese, softened

1 cup grated Parmesan cheese

1/2 cup mayonnaise

1 teaspoon garlic salt

1 teaspoon lemon juice

1/2 teaspoon Old Bay seasoning

1/2 teaspoon pepper

Tabasco sauce to taste

2 (14-ounce) cans water-pack artichoke hearts, drained, chopped

Toast points or crackers

Squeeze the excess moisture from the spinach. Combine the cream cheese, Parmesan cheese, mayonnaise, garlic salt, lemon juice, Old Bay seasoning, pepper and Tabasco sauce in a bowl and mix well. Stir in the artichokes. Fold in the spinach.

Spoon the spinach mixture into a baking dish. Bake at 350 degrees for 20 to 25 minutes or until bubbly. Serve hot with toast points or assorted party crackers.

Serves 12 to 15

* * * * * * * * * * * * * * * * * * * *

Simple Pesto

Combine 2 cups packed fresh basil, 1/2 cup crushed garlic, 1/2 cup grated Parmesan cheese and 1/2 cup grated Romano cheese in a food processor fitted with a steel blade. Process until finely chopped. Add 1/3 cup toasted pine nuts and 3/4 cup olive oil. Pulse until combined. Add another 1/3 cup toasted pine nuts and pulse until chopped. Combine the pesto with hot cooked pasta and 2 tablespoons cream and toss to coat.

Hot Crab Dip

2 tablespoons butter or
margarine
2 medium shallots, minced
1 tablespoon water
1 1/2 teaspoons dry mustard
3/4 teaspoon Old Bay
seasoning
1/2 teaspoon cayenne pepper
1/4 teaspoon red pepper
flakes

1 cup half-and-half
8 ounces cream cheese,
cut into pieces
1 3/4 cups coarsely shredded
white Cheddar cheese
3 tablespoons lemon juice
2 teaspoons Worcestershire
sauce
10 ounces fresh or canned
lump crab meat

1/4 cup chopped fresh
parsley
2 slices white bread, crusts
trimmed, crumbled
1 tablespoon butter or
margarine
1/2 teaspoon paprika
1/4 cup chopped fresh
parsley

Heat 2 tablespoons butter in a saucepan over medium heat until melted. Stir in the shallots. Cook for 2 minutes or until tender, stirring frequently. Add the water and mix well. Simmer for 30 seconds. Stir in the next 4 ingredients. Add the half-and-half and mix well. Bring to a simmer. Add the cream cheese and Cheddar cheese gradually, whisking constantly. Simmer for 2 minutes, whisking constantly. Remove from heat. Stir in the lemon juice and Worcestershire sauce. Add the crab meat and 1/4 cup parsley.

Spoon the crab meat mixture into a baking dish. Sprinkle with the bread crumbs and dot with 1 tablespoon butter. Sprinkle with the paprika. Place the baking dish on the center oven rack. Bake at 400 degrees for 25 minutes or until the dip is bubbly and the bread crumbs are golden brown. Sprinkle with 1/4 cup parsley. Serve hot with assorted party crackers or toasted garlic bread.

Serves 10 to 12

* *

Bacon-Wrapped Shrimp

Slice whole pickled jalapeño chiles horizontally into halves and rinse. Cut sliced Pepper Jack cheese into 1/4-inch strips and sliced bacon horizontally into halves. Wrap 1 peeled deveined large shrimp, 1 cheese strip and 1 jalapeño chile slice with 1 bacon half and secure with a wooden pick. Arrange on a baking sheet. Broil until the shrimp turn pink and the bacon is crisp, turning frequently.

The Big Dipper

1 (15-ounce) can chili
   without beans
1 (15-ounce) can diced
   roasted garlic tomatoes

1 (4-ounce) can green chiles,
   drained
1 1/2 cups cubed process
   cheese

1/2 cup sliced green onions
1/2 teaspoon cayenne
   pepper

Combine the chili, undrained tomatoes, green chiles, cheese, green onions and cayenne pepper in a saucepan and mix well. Cook until the cheese melts, stirring frequently.

Spoon the dip into a chafing dish. Garnish with chopped tomatoes, red bell pepper strips and additional sliced green onions. Serve warm with fresh vegetables, chips and/or toasted French bread slices.

Serves 6 to 8

* *

Guacamole

6 slices bacon
2 medium ripe avocados,
   mashed
1 tablespoon minced onion

1 garlic clove, minced
1 teaspoon cumin
1/4 teaspoon chili powder
1/4 teaspoon salt

1 cup chopped tomato
   (optional)
1/3 cup mayonnaise
Tortilla chips

Fry the bacon in a skillet until crisp; drain. Crumble the bacon. Combine the avocados, onion, garlic, cumin, chili powder and salt in a bowl and mix well. Stir in the bacon, tomato and mayonnaise just before serving. Serve with tortilla chips.

Serves 4 to 6

Marshmallow Dip with Fresh Fruit Kabobs

1/2 cup plain yogurt

4 ounces cream cheese, softened

1/4 cup marshmallow creme

1 (8-ounce) can pineapple chunks, drained

Sections of 1 orange, cut into halves

2 bananas, cut into 1-inch slices

1 pear, cut into chunks

16 maraschino cherries, drained

Combine the yogurt, cream cheese and marshmallow creme in a bowl and mix well. Chill, covered, until serving time.

Thread the pineapple chunks, orange, bananas, pear and cherries alternately on 16 wooden skewers. Arrange the kabobs on a platter surrounding the dip.

Serves 16

* *

Pico de Gallo

1/2 cup white vinegar

1/4 cup vegetable oil

6 medium tomatoes, chopped

1 small red onion, chopped

6 green onions, thinly sliced

1/2 red bell pepper, chopped

1/2 green bell pepper, chopped

1 small jalapeño chile, seeded, minced

Juice of 1 lime

2 garlic cloves, crushed

1 teaspoon cumin

1 teaspoon dried oregano-basil mix

Salt and pepper to taste

Chopped fresh cilantro to taste

Tortilla chips

Combine the vinegar, oil, tomatoes, red onion, green onions, bell peppers, jalapeño chile, lime juice, garlic, cumin, oregano-basil mix, salt, pepper and cilantro in a bowl and mix well. Chill, covered, until serving time. Add chopped avocado for variety. Serve with the chips or as a relish.

Serves 15 to 20

Avocado Pico de Gallo

2 tomatoes, chopped
1 cup chopped fresh cilantro
1 (4-ounce) can diced green
   chiles, drained
1/2 small onion, chopped

Juice of 3 limes
1 jalapeño chile, seeded,
   minced
2 teaspoons minced fresh
   garlic

Salt to taste
3 large ripe avocados,
   chopped
Tortilla chips

Combine the tomatoes, cilantro, green chiles, onion, lime juice, jalapeño chile and garlic in a bowl and mix gently. Season with salt. Stir in the avocados just before serving. Serve with tortilla chips.
   Serves 10 to 12

* * * * * * * * * * * * * * * * * * * *

Texas Caviar

1/2 cup (1 stick) butter
1 garlic clove, minced
1 tablespoon chopped
   green onions

1 (16-ounce) can jalapeño
   black-eyed peas,
   drained, mashed
1 (5-ounce) jar Old English
   cheese spread

1 (4-ounce) can diced green
   chiles, drained
Tortilla chips

Heat the butter in a saucepan until melted. Add the garlic and green onions. Sauté until the green onions are tender. Stir in the black-eyed peas, cheese spread and green chiles.
   Cook until the cheese melts, stirring frequently. Spoon into a chafing dish. Serve hot with tortilla chips.
   Serves 10 to 12

Almond Mushroom Pâté

1 1/2 cups sliced mushrooms
1/4 cup chopped onion
1 garlic clove, chopped
2 tablespoons margarine

1/2 teaspoon tarragon
1 cup slivered almonds
2 tablespoons cream cheese

1 tablespoon lemon juice
2 teaspoons soy sauce
1/8 teaspoon white pepper

Sauté the mushrooms, onion and garlic in the margarine in a large skillet until the mushrooms and onion are tender but not brown. Stir in the tarragon.

Spoon the mushroom mixture into a food processor container. Add the almonds, cream cheese, lemon juice, soy sauce and white pepper. Process until smooth. Spoon the pâté into a crock or bowl. Serve with assorted party crackers.

Serves 4 to 6

* *

Chef's Cheese Ring

1 pound Cheddar cheese,
    shredded
1 cup reduced-fat
    mayonnaise

1 cup chopped pecans
1 bunch green onions, finely
    chopped

Cayenne pepper to taste
1/2 cup strawberry preserves
Butter-flavor crackers

Combine the cheese, mayonnaise, pecans, green onions and cayenne pepper in a bowl and mix well. Mound the cheese mixture on a serving platter.

Make a well in the center of the cheese mound. Spoon the preserves into the well. Serve with butter-flavor crackers.

Serves 8 to 10

Roquefort Torte

Grated Parmesan cheese to taste

Dried bread crumbs or finely chopped nuts

12 ounces bacon or turkey bacon

1 small onion, chopped

32 ounces cream cheese, softened, chopped

8 ounces Roquefort cheese or bleu cheese, crumbled

4 eggs

2 1/2 tablespoons Worcestershire sauce

1 tablespoon Tabasco sauce

Spray the bottom of a springform pan with nonstick cooking spray. Coat with a mixture of Parmesan cheese and bread crumbs.

Process the bacon and onion in a food processor until finely chopped. Sauté the bacon mixture in a skillet until the bacon is crisp; drain. Combine the cream cheese, Roquefort cheese, eggs, Worcestershire sauce and Tabasco sauce in a mixing bowl. Beat until blended. Stir in the bacon mixture.

Spoon the cream cheese mixture into the prepared springform pan. Bake at 350 degrees for 1 hour. Turn off the oven. Let the torte stand in the oven for 1 hour. Cool in pan on a wire rack. Serve with fresh strawberries and baguette slices.

The torte may be prepared in advance and stored, covered, in the freezer. Reheat before serving or serve at room temperature.

Serves 20 to 25

* * * * * * * * * * * * * * * * * * * *

Pistachio Smoked Salmon Spread

8 ounces cream cheese, softened

3 ounces smoked salmon, flaked or finely chopped

1/4 cup chopped pistachios

1 tablespoon lemon juice

Beat the cream cheese in a mixing bowl until light and fluffy. Stir in the salmon, pistachios and lemon juice. Serve with croissants or brioche.

Serves 6

Shrimp Mold

8 ounces cream cheese
1 (10-ounce) can tomato
　soup
1 1/2 envelopes unflavored
　gelatin

1/2 cup cold water
1 pound chopped cooked
　shrimp

1 1/2 ribs celery, chopped
1 cup mayonnaise
1/2 cup chopped onion

Combine the cream cheese and soup in a saucepan. Heat until blended, stirring frequently. Soften the gelatin in the cold water.

Stir the gelatin mixture, shrimp, celery, mayonnaise and onion into the hot soup mixture. Spoon the shrimp mixture into a mold. Chill until set. Invert onto a lettuce-lined serving platter. Serve with assorted party crackers.

Serves 12 to 15

* *

Shrimply Delicious Spread

32 ounces cream cheese,
　softened
2 (10-ounce) cans tomatoes
　with green chiles
1 onion, finely chopped

1 green bell pepper, finely
　chopped
1 tablespoon Worcestershire
　sauce

1 teaspoon salt
1 teaspoon cayenne pepper
4 (4-ounce) cans shrimp,
　drained, chopped

Combine the cream cheese, undrained tomatoes, onion, bell pepper, Worcestershire sauce, salt and cayenne pepper in a bowl and mix well. Fold in the shrimp. Serve at room temperature with assorted party crackers.

Serves 15 to 20

Bruschetta

6 Roma tomatoes, seeded,
    finely chopped
6 to 8 basil leaves, minced

1 small red onion, finely
    chopped
2 small garlic cloves, minced

1/2 cup balsamic vinegar
1/4 cup extra-virgin olive oil
1 baguette, sliced

Combine the tomatoes, basil, onion, garlic, balsamic vinegar and olive oil in a bowl and mix gently. Chill, covered, in the refrigerator for up to 2 hours, stirring occasionally.

Slice the baguette into 1/4-inch slices, discarding the ends. Arrange the slices in a single layer on a baking sheet. Spray lightly with nonstick cooking spray or olive oil nonstick cooking spray. Toast at 375 degrees for 8 to 10 minutes or until light brown. Remove to a wire rack to cool. Serve the tomato mixture with the bruschetta. May substitute toast points or crackers for the baguette slices.

Serves 10 to 12

* * * * * * * * * * * * * * * * * * * *

Savory Cheese Toast

8 slices (any type) bread,
    crusts trimmed
1 cup shredded sharp
    Cheddar cheese
8 slices bacon, crisp-cooked,
    crumbled

1 small onion, grated
1/3 cup mayonnaise
1 egg, beaten
1/2 teaspoon Worcestershire
    sauce
1/8 teaspoon dry mustard

8 dashes of Tabasco sauce
Freshly ground pepper
    to taste
Paprika to taste

Toast the bread in a toaster. Combine the cheese, bacon, onion, mayonnaise, egg, Worcestershire sauce, dry mustard, Tabasco sauce and pepper in a bowl and mix well.

Spread each bread slice with 1/8 of the cheese mixture. Sprinkle with paprika. Cut each slice into 3 long strips or 4 squares. Arrange the strips or squares in a single layer on a baking sheet. Chill, covered, in the refrigerator.

Let the cheese toast stand at room temperature for 30 minutes. Bake at 350 degrees for 20 minutes. Serve warm. May be prepared up to 1 day in advance and stored in the refrigerator, or freeze for future use. Bake just before serving.

Makes 24 to 30

Cucumber Sandwiches

8 ounces cream cheese,
   softened

1/3 cup mayonnaise

1 medium cucumber, peeled,
   seeded, finely chopped

1/2 teaspoon chopped fresh
   dillweed

1/4 teaspoon garlic salt

20 thin slices white sandwich
   bread

20 thin slices whole wheat
   sandwich bread

Process the cream cheese and mayonnaise in a food processor until smooth, scraping the side of the bowl occasionally. Stir in the cucumber, dillweed and garlic salt.

Spread the cucumber mixture on 1 side of each slice of white bread. Top with the whole wheat bread. Trim the crusts and cut the sandwiches diagonally into halves. You may cut the sandwiches with large cookie cutters of your choice for variety.

Serves 40

* *

Black Bean and Cheese Spirals

1 cup drained canned
   black beans

1/2 cup salsa

4 (8-inch) flour tortillas

4 ounces Monterey Jack
   cheese, shredded

1 cup finely chopped green,
   red or yellow bell pepper

Mash 1/2 cup of the beans in a bowl. Stir in the salsa and remaining beans. Spread 1/4 of the bean mixture on 1 side of each tortilla. Sprinkle with the cheese and bell pepper. Roll tightly to enclose the filling.

Wrap each tortilla roll tightly in plastic wrap. Chill in the refrigerator. Cut each tortilla roll into 8 slices just before serving.

Makes 32 spirals

Tricolor Pepper Wedges

8 ounces cream cheese,
    softened

1 cup sour cream

1 (2-ounce) jar diced
    pimentos, drained

8 ounces hot pepper
    Monterey Jack cheese,
    shredded

1/4 cup chopped black
    olives

1/4 cup sliced green onions

1 medium green bell pepper

1 medium red bell pepper

1 medium yellow bell pepper

Combine the cream cheese and sour cream in a mixing bowl. Beat at medium speed until smooth, scraping the bowl frequently. Stir in the pimentos, Monterey Jack cheese, olives and green onions. Chill, covered, for 2 hours or longer.

Cut a 1-inch circle around the stem of each bell pepper and remove the stems. Discard the seeds from the stems, reserving the stems. Scoop out the seeds and membranes from the inside of the bell peppers with a spoon. Spoon the cream cheese mixture into the bell peppers. Top with the reserved stems. Wrap each filled bell pepper in plastic wrap or place in individual sealable plastic bags. Chill for 2 hours or longer.

To serve, remove and discard the pepper stems. Cut each stuffed pepper lengthwise into halves. Cut each half into 4 wedges. Arrange the wedges on a tray. Garnish with sliced olives and pimento strips. You may prepare up to 1 day in advance and chill, covered, in the refrigerator. Cut just before serving.

Makes 2 dozen wedges

* * * * * * * * * * * * * * * * * * * *

Stuffed Jalapeños

For a quick and easy appetizer, drain and rinse 1 can of whole jalapeño chiles. Remove the stems and slice horizontally into halves; discard the seeds. Spread softened cream cheese in each jalapeño half. Sprinkle with pecan pieces and arrange on a serving platter.

Chicken Pot Stickers

2 cups finely chopped green
    cabbage
2 teaspoons vegetable oil
1/2 cup water
8 ounces ground cooked
    chicken

1/3 cup minced green onions
1 tablespoon grated
    gingerroot
1 garlic clove, crushed
1/2 teaspoon salt
1/2 teaspoon sesame oil

1 egg white, lightly beaten
2 dozen won ton wrappers
2 teaspoons cornstarch
4 teaspoons vegetable oil
1 cup water

Sauté the cabbage in 2 teaspoons oil in a large skillet for 7 to 9 minutes or just until the cabbage begins to brown, adding 1/2 cup water during the process to prevent the cabbage from sticking. Transfer the cabbage to a bowl to cool.

Stir the ground chicken, green onions, gingerroot, garlic, salt, sesame oil and egg white into the cabbage and mix well. Spoon 1 teaspoon of the cabbage mixture onto the center of each won ton wrapper. Moisten the edges with water, bring the opposite corners to the center and pinch to seal. Arrange the won tons on a baking sheet sprinkled with the cornstarch. Cover with a damp tea towel to prevent drying out.

Heat 2 teaspoons of the 4 teaspoons oil in a skillet. Add half the won tons. Cook for 3 minutes or until the bottoms are light brown. Add 1/2 cup of the water to the skillet. Cook, covered, for 3 to 4 minutes longer or until the water is absorbed. Remove to a paper towel to drain.

Wipe the skillet with a paper towel. Repeat the cooking process with the remaining oil, remaining won tons and remaining water. Serve hot with hot mustard or Chinese dipping sauce. To prevent the won tons from opening during the cooking process brush with beaten egg white.

Makes 2 dozen pot stickers

Crab Puffs

1 (7-ounce) can crab meat, or 8 ounces fresh crab meat, drained
8 ounces cream cheese, softened

2 tablespoons bread crumbs
2 tablespoons grated onion
2 drops of sesame oil

Garlic powder to taste
3 dozen won ton wrappers
Peanut oil for frying

Combine the crab meat, cream cheese, bread crumbs, onion, sesame oil and garlic powder in a bowl and mix well. Spoon 1 teaspoon of the crab meat mixture onto the center of each won ton wrapper. Fold over 1 corner to the center. Moisten the remaining corners and fold into the center; press to seal.

Pour enough peanut oil into a skillet or deep fryer to cover 5 to 6 crab puffs. Deep-fry in batches for 3 minutes or until brown. Drain on paper towels. Serve the crab puffs with hot mustard or sweet-and-sour sauce. The crab puffs may be prepared in advance and frozen for future use. Reheat before serving.

Makes 3 dozen crab puffs

* * * * * * * * * * * * * * * * * * *

Crab-Stuffed Mushrooms

1 pound crab meat, drained
1/3 cup chopped black olives
5 tablespoons mayonnaise
2 tablespoons chopped fresh parsley

1 green onion, minced
1 tablespoon lemon juice
1/2 teaspoon Dijon mustard
1/4 teaspoon garlic powder
2 dozen large mushrooms

1/2 cup chicken broth or white wine
Grated Parmesan cheese to taste

Combine the crab meat, olives, mayonnaise, parsley, green onion, lemon juice, Dijon mustard and garlic powder in a bowl and mix well.

Remove the stems from the mushrooms and discard or save for another recipe. Stuff the mushroom caps with the crab meat mixture. Arrange the mushrooms stuffing side up in a heavy baking pan. Pour the broth over the mushrooms. Sprinkle generously with cheese. Bake, covered with foil, at 400 degrees for 15 minutes. Remove the foil. Bake for 5 minutes longer or until light brown.

Makes 2 dozen mushrooms

Stuffed Mushrooms

1 (10-ounce) package frozen
   chopped spinach,
   thawed, drained
4 ounces Monterey Jack
   cheese, shredded

1 cup sour cream
1/4 cup (1/2 stick) butter,
   softened
Chopped green onions
   to taste

3 pounds large mushrooms,
   stems removed
Paprika

Squeeze the excess moisture from the spinach. Combine the spinach, cheese, sour cream, butter and green onions in a bowl and mix well. Shape the spinach mixture into balls to fit the mushrooms caps. Place the stuffing balls in the mushroom caps.

Arrange the stuffed mushrooms in a baking dish sprayed with nonstick cooking spray. Sprinkle with paprika. Bake at 350 degrees for 15 minutes or until bubbly. You may substitute chopped artichoke hearts for the spinach.

Serves 12 to 15

* * * * * * * * * * * * * * * * * * * *

Pepperoni Calzone

1/2 cup grated Parmesan
   cheese
1 egg, beaten
1/2 teaspoon parsley flakes
1/4 teaspoon garlic salt

1/4 teaspoon oregano
1/8 teaspoon pepper
1 loaf frozen bread dough,
   thawed

1 package sliced pepperoni
4 ounces provolone cheese,
   shredded
Butter to taste

Combine the Parmesan cheese, egg, parsley flakes, garlic salt, oregano and pepper in a bowl and mix well. Pat the bread dough into a rectangle on a greased baking sheet. Spread the Parmesan cheese mixture over the top of the dough to the edges. Sprinkle with the pepperoni and provolone cheese. Roll as for a jelly roll.

Bake at 350 degrees for 35 minutes, covering if needed during the last 10 minutes of baking to prevent overbrowning. Brush with butter. Slice and serve. You may microwave the pepperoni for a short amount of time and pat with a paper towel to help remove excess fat.

Serves 8 to 10

Smoked Salmon

SALMON

8 cups boiling water

2/3 cup sea salt

1/2 cup packed brown sugar

1 (6-pound) salmon fillet

*F*OR THE SALMON, combine the boiling water, sea salt and brown sugar in a heatproof bowl to make a brine. Let stand until room temperature. Pour the brine over the salmon in a large container. Chill, covered, for 8 to 12 hours; drain. Rinse the salmon with cool water and pat dry.

Heat a smoker to 275 to 300 degrees. Arrange the salmon skin side down in the smoker. Smoke for 1 1/2 to 2 hours or until the salmon flakes easily at the thinnest point. Let stand until room temperature.

TARRAGON SAUCE

1/3 cup mayonnaise

1/3 cup sour cream

1/3 cup minced onion

1 1/2 teaspoons chopped fresh tarragon, or 1/2 teaspoon dried tarragon

1/4 teaspoon lemon juice

White pepper to taste

The flavor is best if served after cooling to room temperature but the salmon may be stored, covered, in the refrigerator for future use. If a smoker is not available, the salmon may be smoked in an oven by placing a pan of water with mesquite chips on the rack below the salmon.

*F*OR THE SAUCE, combine the mayonnaise, sour cream, onion, tarragon, lemon juice and white pepper in a bowl and mix well. Serve with the salmon.

Serves 12 to 15

* * * * * * * * * * * * * * * * * * *

Homemade Hot Cocoa Mix

For a great holiday gift idea, package the cocoa mix in a decorative tin or include in a holiday gift basket with a couple of mugs. Mix 2 cups nonfat dry milk powder, 1 cup sugar, 3/4 cup nondairy creamer, 1/2 cup baking cocoa and 1/2 teaspoon salt and store in a jar with a tight-fitting lid. To serve, combine 1/4 cup of the cocoa mix and 3/4 cup boiling water in a mug and stir. Serve with cinnamon sticks and/or marshmallows.

Amaretto Freeze

1 to 2 quarts vanilla ice
cream

1/3 cup amaretto
1/4 cup crème de cacao

2 tablespoons Triple Sec

Place 1 quart of the ice cream in a blender container. Add the amaretto, crème de cacao and Triple Sec. Process until smooth. Add as much of the remaining 1 quart ice cream as the blender will hold. Process until blended.

Store in the freezer until just before serving time; thawing time may be required. Spoon into tall fluted glasses.

Serves 6

* *

Brandy Slush

7 cups water
1 1/2 cups sugar
1 (12-ounce) can frozen
lemonade concentrate,
thawed

1 (12-ounce) can frozen
orange juice concentrate,
thawed

1 1/2 cups brandy
Lemon-lime soda

Combine the water and sugar in a saucepan. Bring to a boil, stirring occasionally. Boil until the sugar dissolves. Remove from heat. Let stand until cool.

Stir the lemonade concentrate, orange juice concentrate and brandy into the sugar syrup. Pour into a freezer container. Freeze for 24 hours.

To serve, fill glasses halfway with the slush mixture. Top off with the soda and stir. May place the slush mixture in an ice bucket while serving to keep cool.

Makes 24 (8-ounce) servings

Frozen Cranberry Margaritas

3 (12-ounce) cans frozen cranberry juice concentrate

2 (12-ounce) cans frozen limeade concentrate

1 (12-ounce) can frozen orange juice concentrate

9 to 10 concentrate cans water

1 concentrate can Triple Sec

1 liter tequila, or to taste

Confectioners' sugar to taste

Combine the cranberry juice concentrate, limeade concentrate, orange juice concentrate, water, Triple Sec and tequila in a large freezer container and mix well. Freeze for 2 to 3 days.

To serve, let the frozen cranberry mixture stand at room temperature for 1 to 2 hours; mixture should be slushy. Moisten the rims of margarita glasses and dip in confectioners' sugar, rotating gently to cover the rims evenly. Pour the slush mixture into the prepared glasses.

Serves 25 to 30

* *

Watermelon Slushies

2 cups chopped seeded watermelon, frozen

1 (6-ounce) can frozen lemonade concentrate

2 tablespoons confectioners' sugar

Ice cubes

Sugar to taste

Combine the watermelon, lemonade concentrate and confectioners' sugar in a blender container. Fill the blender container with ice and add just enough water to blend. Process until blended, adding additional ice and water until the blender is full.

Dip the rims of margarita glasses in the slush mixture and then dip in sugar, rotating gently to cover the rims evenly. Pour the slush mixture into the glasses. Add 1/2 cup tequila and 1/4 cup Triple Sec for Watermelon Margarita Slushies.

Serves 6 to 8

Frozen Peachy Punch

3 (3-ounce) packages peach
    gelatin
13 cups hot water

4 cups sugar
2 (46-ounce) cans pineapple
    juice

1 cup lemon juice
2 quarts ginger ale, chilled

Dissolve the gelatin in 9 cups of the hot water in a heatproof bowl and stir. Let stand until cool. Dissolve the sugar in the remaining 4 cups hot water in a heatproof bowl and stir. Let stand until cool.

Combine the gelatin mixture, sugar mixture, pineapple juice and lemon juice in a large container and mix well. Pour equal amounts of the punch mixture into two 1-gallon freezer containers. Freeze until firm.

Let the frozen punch mixture stand at room temperature for 3 hours. Add 1 quart of ginger ale to each gallon container and shake to mix. Ladle into punch cups.

Serves 50

* * * * * * * * * * * * * * * * * * *

Sparkling Strawberry Punch

2 (10-ounce) packages
    frozen strawberries
1 (6-ounce) can frozen
    lemonade concentrate

1/4 cup sugar
1 quart rosé, chilled

1 (28-ounce) bottle ginger
    ale, chilled
2 trays ice cubes

Process the strawberries, lemonade concentrate and sugar in a blender until smooth. Pour into a punch bowl. Stir in the wine, ginger ale and ice cubes 10 minutes before serving. Garnish with orange slices. Ladle into punch cups.

Makes 18 (1-cup) servings

True Sangria

2 large oranges, sliced
1 large lemon, sliced
1 cup (heaping) sugar
3/4 cup peach brandy

1 (4-liter) bottle burgundy, such as Carlo Rossi or Gallo

Assorted seasonal fruits, such as nectarines, peaches, cherries and/or strawberries

Layer the oranges and lemon in a large container. Pour the sugar and brandy over the fruit, mashing the fruit to release the juices. Marinate in the refrigerator for 1 to 2 days.

Add the wine to the brandy mixture and mix well. Stir in assorted fresh fruits. Marinate in the refrigerator for 2 days or longer. Pour into glasses.

Serves 20 to 25

* *

Wassail

6 cinnamon sticks
6 tablespoons whole ginger
3 tablespoons whole cloves
6 cups apple cider

4 1/2 cups cranberry juice
3 cups orange juice
3 cups pineapple juice

3 cups water
1 1/2 cups lemon juice
1 1/2 cups sugar

Tie the cinnamon sticks, ginger and cloves in a cheesecloth bag. Combine the apple cider, cranberry juice, orange juice, pineapple juice, water, lemon juice and sugar in a stockpot. Add the spice bag and simmer until serving time. Discard the spice bag. Ladle into mugs.

Serves 25 to 30

Basic Substitutions

If the recipe calls for	You can substitute

Flour

1 cup sifted all-purpose flour	1 cup less 2 tablespoons unsifted all-purpose flour
1 cup sifted cake flour	1 cup less 2 tablespoons sifted all-purpose flour
1 cup sifted self-rising flour	1 cup sifted all-purpose flour plus $1^1/_2$ teaspoons baking powder and a pinch of salt

Milk/Cream

1 cup buttermilk	1 cup plain yogurt, or 1 tablespoon lemon juice or vinegar plus enough milk to measure 1 cup; let stand for 5 minutes before using
1 cup whipping cream or half-and-half	$^7/_8$ cup whole milk plus $1^1/_2$ tablespoons butter
1 cup light cream	$^7/_8$ cup whole milk plus 3 tablespoons butter
1 cup sour cream	1 cup plain yogurt
1 cup sour milk	1 cup plain yogurt
1 cup whole milk	1 cup skim or nonfat milk plus 2 tablespoons butter or margarine

Seasonings

1 teaspoon allspice	$^1/_2$ teaspoon cinnamon plus $^1/_8$ teaspoon cloves
1 cup ketchup	1 cup tomato sauce plus $^1/_2$ cup sugar plus 2 tablespoons vinegar
1 teaspoon Italian spice	$^1/_4$ teaspoon each oregano, basil, thyme, rosemary plus dash of cayenne pepper
1 teaspoon lemon juice	$^1/_2$ teaspoon vinegar

Sugar

1 cup confectioners' sugar	$^1/_2$ cup plus 1 tablespoon granulated sugar
1 cup granulated sugar	$1^3/_4$ cups confectioners' sugar, 1 cup packed light brown sugar or $^3/_4$ cup honey

Other

1 package active dry yeast	$^1/_2$ cake compressed yeast
1 teaspoon baking powder	$^1/_4$ teaspoon cream of tartar plus $^1/_4$ teaspoon baking soda
1 cup dry bread crumbs	$^3/_4$ cup cracker crumbs or 1 cup cornflake crumbs
1 cup (2 sticks) butter	$^7/_8$ cup vegetable oil or 1 cup margarine
1 tablespoon cornstarch	2 tablespoons all-purpose flour
1 cup dark corn syrup	$^3/_4$ cup light corn syrup plus $^1/_4$ cup light molasses
1 cup light corn syrup	1 cup maple syrup
$1^2/_3$ ounces semisweet chocolate	1 ounce unsweetened chocolate plus 4 teaspoons granulated sugar
1 ounce unsweetened chocolate	3 tablespoons unsweetened baking cocoa plus 1 tablespoon butter or margarine
1 (1-ounce) square chocolate	$^1/_4$ cup baking cocoa plus 1 teaspoon shortening
1 cup honey	1 to $1^1/_4$ cups sugar plus $^1/_4$ cup liquid, or 1 cup corn syrup or molasses
currants	raisins
1 egg	$^1/_4$ cup mayonnaise

Soups, Stews & Chowders

Any Bean Soup

1 to 2 cups chopped onions
1 cup chopped green onions
1 cup chopped celery with
  leaves
Butter, vegetable oil or
  bacon drippings

1/4 cup chopped fresh
  parsley
1 (1-pound) package navy
  beans, lima beans, split
  peas or lentils
2 quarts water

1 or 2 bay leaves
Ham bone, ham hock or
  bacon drippings
  (optional)
Salt and pepper to taste

Sauté the onions, green onions and celery in butter in a stockpot until the onions are tender. Stir in the parsley. Sauté for 1 minute. Add any variety or combination of sorted and rinsed beans, peas or lentils, water, bay leaves and ham bone.

Bring to a boil; reduce heat. Simmer over low heat until the beans are tender, stirring occasionally. Discard the bay leaves. Season with salt and pepper. Ladle into soup bowls.

Serves 4 to 6

* *

Governor's Broccoli and Cheese Soup

2 tablespoons finely
  chopped white onion
2 tablespoons butter
3 tablespoons flour

Salt and pepper to taste
2 cups milk
1 cup cubed Velveeta cheese

1 (10-ounce) package frozen
  chopped broccoli
1 1/2 cups water
3 chicken bouillon cubes

Sauté the onion in the butter in a stockpot until tender. Stir in the flour, salt and pepper. Cook until blended, stirring constantly. Blend in the milk. Cook until thickened, stirring constantly. Stir in the cheese. Cook until the cheese melts, stirring constantly. Remove from heat.

Combine the broccoli, water and bouillon cubes in a microwave-safe dish. Microwave for 7 minutes or until the broccoli is tender. Add the undrained broccoli mixture to the stockpot and mix well. Cook just until heated through, stirring frequently. Ladle into soup bowls. This recipe is similar to a recipe served at the Governor's residence in Des Moines, Iowa.

Serves 2 to 4

Contributed by Maple Place Bed & Breakfast

Cowboy Soup

2 pounds ground beef
1 medium onion, chopped
2 (15-ounce) cans Mexican-
style tomatoes
2 (14-ounce) cans pinto
beans

2 (14-ounce) cans kidney
beans
1 (14-ounce) can whole
kernel corn
4 (4-ounce) cans chopped
green chiles

1 envelope taco
seasoning mix
1 envelope ranch salad
dressing mix

Brown the ground beef in a stockpot, stirring until crumbly; drain. Add the onion, undrained tomatoes, undrained pinto beans, undrained kidney beans, undrained corn, green chiles, seasoning mix and dressing mix and mix well. Simmer for 1 hour, stirring occasionally. Ladle into soup bowls.

Serves 6 to 8

* *

Green Chile Chicken Soup

3 (10-ounce) cans cream of
chicken soup
1 small white onion,
chopped

3 boneless skinless chicken
breasts, cooked
3 cans green chile enchilada
sauce

1 (16-ounce) can white corn,
drained
1 (4-ounce) can chopped
green chiles, drained

Combine the soup and onion in a large saucepan and mix well. Cook over medium heat for 10 to 15 minutes, stirring occasionally. Cut the chicken into bite-size pieces. Add the chicken, enchilada sauce, corn and green chiles 1 at a time, stirring well after each addition. Bring to a boil; reduce heat.

Simmer for 30 minutes, stirring occasionally. Ladle into soup bowls. Serve with baked tortilla chips, chopped red bell pepper and shredded pepper Jack cheese. Substitute 1 soup can chicken broth (saved from boiling the chicken) for 1 of the cans of soup for a thinner consistency.

Makes 10 (1 1/2-cup) servings

Rojo Chicken Tortilla Soup

1 (4-ounce) can chopped
   green chiles, drained
1 small onion, chopped
2 garlic cloves, chopped
1/2 fresh jalapeño chile,
   chopped
2 tablespoons olive oil
2 (14-ounce) cans tomatoes
1 tablespoon chopped fresh
   cilantro

1 teaspoon cumin
1 teaspoon chili powder
1 teaspoon Worcestershire
   sauce
1/2 teaspoon sugar
1 (14-ounce) can clear beef
   broth
1 (14-ounce) can clear
   chicken broth

1 (10-ounce) can tomato
   soup
2 cups chopped cooked
   chicken
Shredded Cheddar cheese to
   taste
Tortilla chips
1 avocado, chopped
Sour cream

Sauté the green chiles, onion, garlic and jalapeño chile in the olive oil in a stockpot until the onion is tender. Combine the onion mixture, undrained tomatoes, cilantro, cumin, chili powder, Worcestershire sauce and sugar in a blender container. Process until almost smooth. Pour into a stockpot.

Add the beef broth, chicken broth and tomato soup and mix well. Bring to a boil; reduce heat. Simmer, covered, for 1 hour, stirring occasionally. May be frozen at this point for future use.

Divide the chicken in equal amounts among 6 to 8 soup bowls. Ladle the hot soup over the chicken. Top each serving with shredded cheese, tortilla chips, chopped avocado and sour cream.

Serves 6 to 8

* * * * * * * * * * * * * * * * * * * *

The Junior Welfare League of Enid was officially founded in the fall of 1930 at the beginning of the Depression, and ever since it has provided for the community needs of Enid. Periodically since 1938, JWL has held the "Follies." In 1939, Will Rogers performed at the Follies to a packed Convention Hall, and $780.90 was raised.

Blue Ribbon Chili

2 pounds fresh Italian sausage
2 cups chopped onions
6 garlic cloves, minced
1 tablespoon olive oil
2 pounds lean ground beef
2 green bell peppers, chopped
2 red bell peppers, chopped

6 fresh jalapeño chiles, seeded, chopped
2 (28-ounce) cans diced tomatoes
1 (28-ounce) can crushed tomatoes
1 (15-ounce) can tomato sauce
1 cup dry red wine

1 cup chopped fresh parsley
2 tablespoons tomato paste
6 tablespoons chili powder
3 tablespoons cumin
2 tablespoons oregano
1 tablespoon basil
2 teaspoons salt
2 teaspoons pepper
1 1/2 teaspoons fennel seeds

Remove the casings from the sausage. Brown the sausage in a large skillet over medium heat, stirring until crumbly. Drain on a paper towel. Sauté the onions and garlic in the olive oil in a stockpot until the onions are tender. Add the ground beef and mix well. Cook for 15 minutes or until the ground beef is brown and crumbly, stirring frequently; drain.

Add the sausage, bell peppers and jalapeño chiles to the ground beef mixture and mix well. Cook for 15 minutes, stirring occasionally. Stir in the undrained tomatoes, tomato sauce, wine, parsley, tomato paste, chili powder, cumin, oregano, basil, salt, pepper and fennel seeds.

Simmer for 1 1/2 hours or until of the desired consistency, stirring frequently. Ladle into chili bowls. The flavor of the chili is enhanced if prepared 1 day in advance and stored, covered, in the refrigerator. Reheat before serving.

Serves 8 to 10

Chipotle Chili

2 large onions, chopped
3 tablespoons olive oil
10 garlic cloves, minced
2 pounds beef, cut into bite-
    size pieces
3 tablespoons chili powder
2 teaspoons oregano

1 teaspoon cumin
1 teaspoon paprika
2 1/2 cups broth
1 1/2 cups beer
3 tablespoons puréed
    chipotle chiles in adobo
    sauce

1 (6-ounce) can tomato paste
2 teaspoons salt
1 teaspoon sugar
2 (16-ounce) cans kidney
    beans, drained (optional)

Sauté the onions in the olive oil in a stockpot over medium heat for 4 minutes. Stir in the garlic. Sauté for 1 minute. Add the beef and mix well. Cook over medium-high heat until the beef is brown, turning occasionally. Add the chili powder, oregano, cumin and paprika and stir until the beef is evenly coated.

Add the broth, beer, puréed chipotle chiles, tomato paste, salt and sugar to the beef mixture and mix well. Bring to a boil; reduce heat. Simmer, covered, for 1 hour, stirring occasionally. Add the beans and mix well.

Cook just until heated through, stirring frequently. Taste and adjust seasonings. Ladle into chili bowls. Canned chipotle chiles are located in the Mexican food section of most supermarkets.

Serves 6 to 8

* *

Weights and Measures

3 teaspoons = 1 tablespoon
4 tablespoons = 1/4 cup
5 1/3 tablespoons = 1/3 cup
8 tablespoons = 1/2 cup
10 2/3 tablespoons = 2/3 cup
12 tablespoons = 3/4 cup
16 tablespoons = 1 cup
1 tablespoon = 1/2 fluid ounce
1 cup = 8 fluid ounces
1 cup = 1/2 pint

2 cups = 1 pint
4 cups = 1 quart
2 pints = 1 quart
4 quarts = 1 gallon
1 tablespoon = 14.79 milliliters
1 cup = 236.6 milliliters
1.06 quarts = 1 liter
1 pound = 453.59 grams
1 ounce = 28.35 grams

Wyoming Chili

1 pound ground beef
1 large red bell pepper, chopped
8 ounces fresh mushrooms, sliced
1/2 large white onion, chopped
2 garlic cloves, chopped
1 (16-ounce) can chili beans
1 (16-ounce) can kidney beans
1 (16-ounce) can black beans
1 (15-ounce) can tomato sauce
1 tomato sauce can water
2 tablespoons chopped fresh cilantro
1 teaspoon red pepper
1 teaspoon cumin
1 teaspoon oregano
Salt and black pepper to taste
Corn chips
Shredded cheese

Brown the ground beef with the bell pepper, mushrooms, onion and garlic in a skillet, stirring until the ground beef is crumbly; drain. Combine the ground beef mixture, undrained beans, tomato sauce, water, cilantro, red pepper, cumin, oregano, salt and black pepper in a stockpot and mix well.

Bring the chili to a boil; reduce heat. Simmer for 2 hours, stirring occasionally. Ladle the chili over corn chips and shredded cheese in chili bowls. The longer the chili simmers the better the flavor.

Serves 8 to 10

* *

Cool Cucumber Soup

Peel, seed and chop 2 cucumbers. Combine the cucumbers, 2 (15-ounce) cans chicken broth and 1 crushed garlic clove in a 2-quart saucepan. Bring to a boil; reduce heat. Simmer for 30 minutes, stirring occasionally. Let stand until cool. Stir in 2 cups buttermilk. Process the soup in a blender until smooth. Ladle into soup bowls and sprinkle with minced fresh chives.

Monterey Bay Clam Chowder

2 (7- to 10-ounce) cans minced clams

2 cups milk

1 cup cream

1/2 cup finely chopped celery

1/2 cup finely chopped carrot

1/3 cup minced onion

1/4 cup thinly sliced leek bulb

3 tablespoons butter

3 tablespoons flour

1 fish bouillon cube

1/2 to 3/4 cup finely chopped potato

1/2 teaspoon salt

1/2 teaspoon thyme

1/4 teaspoon white pepper

3 to 5 drops of Tabasco sauce, or to taste

1/2 teaspoon Worcestershire sauce

Finely minced fresh parsley

Drain the clams, reserving the clams and liquid. Combine the milk and cream in a bowl and mix well. Sauté the celery, carrot, onion and leek in the butter in a 3-quart saucepan for 6 to 8 minutes. Stir in the flour. Cook until bubbly, stirring constantly. Add the milk mixture gradually, stirring constantly. Stir in the bouillon cube. Bring to a boil.

Boil for 1 to 2 minutes, stirring frequently. Stir in the reserved clam liquid, potato, salt, thyme, white pepper and Tabasco sauce. Bring to a boil; reduce heat.

Simmer for 25 to 35 minutes, stirring occasionally. Stir in the reserved clams and Worcestershire sauce. Heat just to the desired serving temperature, stirring occasionally. Stir in parsley or sprinkle over each serving. Ladle into soup bowls. You may increase the butter and flour by 1 tablespoon each for a thicker consistency.

Serves 6 to 8

Cioppino

1 cup chopped onion

1 medium green bell pepper, chopped

1 carrot, peeled, shredded

1/2 cup chopped celery

3 garlic cloves, crushed

3 tablespoons olive oil

2 (16-ounce) cans chopped tomatoes

1 (8-ounce) can tomato sauce

1 teaspoon basil

1 teaspoon salt

1/2 teaspoon pepper

1 bay leaf

1 pound fresh or frozen white fish steaks, cut into bite-size pieces

1 1/2 cups white wine

1 (7- to 10-ounce) can clams

1 (8-ounce) package frozen peeled shrimp

8 ounces fresh or frozen scallops

2 tablespoons minced fresh parsley

Sauté the onion, bell pepper, carrot, celery and garlic in the olive oil in a skillet. Spoon the onion mixture into a stockpot. Stir in the undrained tomatoes, tomato sauce, basil, salt, pepper and bay leaf. Bring to a boil; reduce heat. Simmer, covered, for 2 hours, stirring occasionally. Discard the bay leaf.

Add the white fish, wine, undrained clams, shrimp and scallops to the stew mixture and mix gently. Simmer for 10 to 15 minutes or until the shrimp turn pink and the scallops are tender, stirring occasionally. Ladle into bowls. Sprinkle with the parsley. Serve with hot crusty Italian bread or sourdough bread. Any type of white fish, such as halibut, sea bass or swordfish may be used.

Serves 6 to 8

✳ ✳ ✳ ✳ ✳ ✳ ✳ ✳ ✳ ✳ ✳ ✳ ✳ ✳ ✳ ✳ ✳ ✳ ✳ ✳

Blue Ribbon Biscuits

Sift 3 cups flour, 2 tablespoons baking powder, 1 teaspoon sugar and 1 teaspoon salt into a bowl. Cut in 2/3 cup shortening until crumbly. Stir in 1 1/2 cups milk. Knead the dough on a floured surface. Roll the dough 1/2 inch thick and cut with a biscuit cutter. Bake at 450 degrees for 12 to 15 minutes or until golden brown. Makes 12 to 16 biscuits.

Jambalaya

1 pound chicken pieces
2 cups water
8 ounces smoked sausage,
   cubed
8 ounces cooked ham,
   cubed
1 tablespoon olive oil
1 cup chopped onion

1 cup chopped bell pepper
1 cup chopped celery
1 cup chopped green onions
2 garlic cloves, minced
1 (16-ounce) can diced
   tomatoes
1 teaspoon thyme

1 teaspoon salt
1 teaspoon black pepper
1/4 teaspoon cayenne
   pepper
1 cup instant rice
1 1/2 teaspoons
   Worcestershire sauce

Combine the chicken and 2 cups water in a saucepan. Bring to a boil. Boil until the chicken is tender. Drain, reserving the stock. Chop the chicken into bite-size pieces, discarding the skin and bones.

Sauté the sausage and ham in the olive oil in a large saucepan until light brown. Remove the sausage mixture to a bowl using a slotted spoon and reserving the pan drippings. Sauté the onion, bell pepper, celery, green onions and garlic in the reserved drippings until the onion is tender.

Drain the tomatoes, reserving the juice. Add the tomatoes, thyme, salt, black pepper and cayenne pepper to the onion mixture. Cook for 5 minutes, stirring occasionally. Add the rice and mix well.

Mix the reserved tomato juice, about 1 1/2 cups reserved chicken stock and Worcestershire sauce in a large measuring cup. Add 2 1/2 cups of the mixture to the saucepan. Bring to a boil; reduce heat to low. Stir in the sausage mixture and chicken. Simmer for 30 minutes or until of the desired consistency, stirring occasionally. Ladle into bowls. You may substitute 2 pounds uncooked peeled shrimp for the chicken and water for the chicken stock.

Serves 4 to 6

Lentil Soup

1 1/4 cups lentils
5 cups water
4 slices bacon, chopped
1 leek, finely chopped
1 onion, finely chopped

1 carrot, finely chopped
1 green bell pepper, finely chopped
1 tomato, finely chopped
3 tablespoons butter

3 tablespoons flour
1 (15-ounce) can consommé
1 to 2 tablespoons salt
2 tablespoons vinegar

Sort and rinse the lentils. Combine the lentils and water in a stockpot. Bring to a boil; reduce heat. Simmer for 1 hour, stirring occasionally. Fry the bacon in a skillet until crisp. Discard the bacon, reserving the bacon drippings. Cook the leek, onion, carrot, bell pepper and tomato in the reserved bacon drippings for 5 minutes or until the vegetables are tender, stirring frequently. Add the vegetable mixture to the lentils and mix well. Melt the butter in the same skillet. Add the flour, stirring until smooth. Add the consommé, salt and vinegar. Cook until slightly thickened, stirring constantly. Add to the lentil mixture and mix well. Cook over low heat for 30 minutes or until of the desired consistency, stirring occasionally. Ladle into soup bowls. Serve with a mixed green salad and country bread.

　　Serves 6 to 10

* *

Low-Fat Potato Soup

4 cups chopped potatoes
1 (10-ounce) can chicken broth
1 cup thinly sliced celery
1/2 cup chopped carrot

1/2 cup chopped onion
1 1/2 teaspoons salt
1/8 teaspoon pepper
1/8 teaspoon dillweed

4 cups skim or whole milk
3 1/2 tablespoons flour
2 tablespoons butter
Shredded Cheddar cheese

Combine the potatoes, broth, celery, carrot, onion, salt, pepper and dillweed in a 3-quart saucepan and mix well. Bring to a boil; reduce heat. Simmer, covered, for 15 to 20 minutes or until the vegetables are tender, stirring occasionally. Stir 3 cups of the skim milk into the potato mixture. Cook until heated through, stirring occasionally. Whisk the flour into the remaining 1 cup skim milk. Add the flour mixture to the soup, stirring constantly. Cook until thickened and heated through, stirring frequently. Stir in the butter. Ladle into soups bowls. Sprinkle with cheese.

　　Serves 4 to 6

Autumn Pumpkin Soup

1 pound onions, chopped
3 cups sliced fresh
   mushrooms
1/2 cup (1 stick) butter

1/2 cup flour
2 quarts chicken stock
1 (14-ounce) can pumpkin
1 1/2 teaspoons curry powder

Salt and pepper to taste
1/2 cup half-and-half
2 tablespoons honey

Sauté the onions and mushrooms in 1/4 cup of the butter in a large saucepan until the onions are tender. Transfer the undrained onion mixture to a bowl. Heat the remaining 1/4 cup butter in the same saucepan until melted. Add the flour and mix well. Whisk in the stock gradually.

   Cook until thickened, stirring constantly. Stir in the onion mixture, pumpkin, curry powder, salt and pepper. Add the half-and-half and honey and mix well. Cook just until heated through, stirring frequently. Ladle into soup bowls. Garnish each serving with a dollop of sour cream and minced fresh parsley. Serve with hot crusty French bread.

   Serves 10 to 12

* *

Wild Rice and Mushroom Soup

8 ounces fresh button
   mushrooms, sliced
2 green onions, sliced
3 tablespoons butter
1/4 cup flour

2 (15-ounce) cans chicken
   broth
1/2 cup wild rice or long
   grain and wild rice mix,
   cooked

1 cup whipping cream
2 teaspoons sherry
Salt and pepper to taste

Sauté the mushrooms and green onions in the butter in a saucepan until tender. Stir in the flour. Add the broth gradually, stirring constantly. Bring to a boil; reduce heat.

   Stir in the wild rice, whipping cream, sherry, salt and pepper. Simmer just until heated through, stirring frequently. Ladle into soup bowls.

   Serves 4

Tomato Basil Soup

1 1/2 cups finely chopped onions
1 1/2 cups (3 sticks) margarine
1 1/2 cups flour

8 cups chicken broth
3 (28-ounce) cans Italian diced tomatoes
5 3/4 cups water
1 (12-ounce) can tomato juice

1/2 cup cream
2 tablespoons oregano
2 teaspoons basil
5 bay leaves

Sauté the onions in the margarine in a stockpot for 10 minutes. Stir in the flour. Add the broth gradually, stirring constantly. Add the undrained tomatoes, water, tomato juice, cream, oregano, basil and bay leaves and mix well.

Bring to a boil; reduce heat. Simmer for 1 hour, stirring occasionally. Discard the bay leaves. Ladle into soup bowls. You may process the canned tomatoes in a blender or food processor before adding to the soup mixture for a smoother consistency.

Makes 20 (2-cup) servings

* * * * * * * * * * * * * * * * * * * *

Tuscan Tomato Soup

1/4 cup olive oil
1/4 cup (1/2 stick) butter
3 onions, minced
4 carrots, peeled, finely chopped

4 ribs celery, finely chopped
3 quarts canned tomatoes
1/2 cup chopped fresh parsley

6 fresh basil leaves
Salt and freshly ground pepper to taste
Pesto (optional)
Sour cream (optional)

Heat the olive oil and butter in a heavy saucepan until the butter melts. Add the onions, carrots and celery and mix well. Cook for 20 minutes or until the vegetables are tender, stirring frequently. Stir in the undrained tomatoes.

Cook over medium heat for 25 to 30 minutes, stirring occasionally. Add the parsley and basil and mix well. Season with salt and pepper. Cook for 1 minute longer, stirring frequently. Ladle into soup bowls. Top each serving with a dollop of pesto and sour cream. You may substitute 14 chopped peeled ripe large tomatoes for the canned tomatoes.

Serves 8 to 10

Beef Vegetable Soup

1 pound ground beef
1 cup chopped onion
2 garlic cloves, crushed
1 (30-ounce) jar chunky
   spaghetti sauce with
   mushrooms and bell
   peppers

1 (10-ounce) can beef broth
2 cups water
1 cup sliced celery
1 teaspoon sugar
1 teaspoon (or less) salt
1/2 teaspoon freshly ground
   pepper

1 (16-ounce) package frozen
   mixed vegetables
1 (10-ounce) can any variety
   diced tomatoes

Brown the ground beef with the onion and garlic in a large saucepan, stirring until the ground beef is crumbly; drain. Stir in the spaghetti sauce, broth, water, celery, sugar, salt and pepper. Bring to a boil; reduce heat.

Simmer, covered, for 20 minutes, stirring frequently. Stir in the mixed vegetables and undrained tomatoes. Bring to a boil; reduce heat. Simmer, covered, for 10 minutes, stirring occasionally. Ladle into soup bowls. The soup is better the next day as the additional time allows the flavors to mellow.

Makes 6 (2-cup) servings

* * * * * * * * * * * * * * * * * * * *

Cattle were first driven from San Antonio, Texas, to Abilene, Kansas, on the Chisholm Trail in 1867. A distance of about eight hundred miles, the Chisholm Trail ran directly through Enid. Many of the cowboy tales still told today happened on the Chisholm Trail, established in 1865 by Jesse Chisholm, a half-Cherokee Indian. Some eight to twelve million cattle came over the Chisholm Trail during the next twenty years. Boarding Kansas railroads, these cattle were then shipped to the beef-starved Northwest where they sold for up to thirteen times as much per head.

Cooking Terms

Al dente: Describes spaghetti or other pasta that is cooked only until it offers a slight resistance to the bite.

Baste: To moisten foods during cooking with pan drippings or a special sauce in order to add flavor and prevent drying.

Beat: To make a mixture smooth by briskly whipping or stirring it with a spoon, wire whisk, rotary beater, or electric mixer.

Blanch: To partially cook fruits, vegetables, or nuts in boiling water or steam to prepare for canning or freezing.

Blend: To process foods in an electric blender.

Braise: To cook food slowly in a small amount of liquid in a tightly covered pan on the range top or in the oven.

Butterfly: To split foods such as shrimp or steak through the middle without completely separating the halves, then spreading the halves to resemble a butterfly.

Coat: To evenly cover food with crumbs, flour, or a batter.

Crisp-tender: Describes vegetables cooked until they are just tender but still somewhat crisp.

Cut in: To combine shortening with dry ingredients using a pastry blender or two knives.

Dash: An ingredient measure that equals about half of $1/8$ teaspoon.

Dissolve: To stir a dry substance in a liquid, such as sugar in coffee or gelatin in water, until no solids remain. Heating the liquid is sometimes necessary.

Dollop: To place a scoop or spoonful of a semi-liquid food, such as whipped cream or sour cream, on top of another food.

Fillet: To cut lean meat or fish into pieces without bones.

Flake: To break food gently into small pieces.

Fold: To gently mix ingredients, using a folding motion. With a spatula, cut down through the mixture; cut across the bottom of the bowl, then up and over, close to the surface. Turn the bowl frequently for even distribution.

Garnish: To add visual appeal to finished food by decorating it with small pieces of food or edible flowers.

Glaze: To brush a mixture on a food to give it a glossy appearance or a hard finish.

Grind: To use a food grinder or food processor to cut food such as meat or fruit into fine pieces.

Knead: To work dough with the heel of your hand in a pressing and folding motion.

Melt: To heat a solid food, such as margarine or sugar, until it is a liquid.

Mix: To stir, usually with a spoon, until ingredients are thoroughly combined.

Mull: To slowly heat beverages, such as red wine or cider, with spices and sugar.

Panbroil: To cook meats in a skillet without added fat, removing any fat as it accumulates.

Panfry: To cook meats, poultry, or fish in a small amount of hot fat.

Partially set: Describes a gelatin mixture chilled until its consistency resembles unbeaten egg whites.

Peel: To remove the outer layer or skin from a fruit or vegetable.

Pit: To remove the seed from a piece of fruit.

Preheat: To heat an oven to the recommended temperature before baking in it.

Process: To blend a food in a food processor. Also refers to the technique of canning foods.

Purée: To chop food into a liquid or heavy paste, usually in a blender, food processor, or food mill.

Reduce: To boil liquids such as pan juices or sauces rapidly so that some of the liquid evaporates, thickening the mixture.

Roast: To cook meats, uncovered, in the oven.

Sauté: To cook or brown food in a small amount of hot fat.

Score: To cut narrow grooves or slits partway through the outer surface of a food.

Shuck: To remove the shells or husks from foods such as oysters, clams, or corn.

Sift: To put one or more dry ingredients through a sifter or sieve to incorporate air and break up any lumps.

Skim: To remove melted fat or other substances from the surface of a liquid.

Stew: To cook food in liquid for a long time until tender, usually in a covered pot.

Stir: To mix ingredients with a spoon in a circular or figure-8 motion until combined.

Whip: To beat food lightly and rapidly using a wire whisk, rotary beater, or electric mixer to incorporate air into the mixture and increase its volume.

Salads

Fresh Cranberry Relish

1 (16-ounce) can juice-pack crushed pineapple

1 (11-ounce) can mandarin oranges

1 (16-ounce) package fresh cranberries

1 cup sugar

1 (6-ounce) package raspberry gelatin

Drain the pineapple and mandarin oranges, reserving the juices separately. Process the cranberries in a food processor until ground. Combine the cranberries, sugar and reserved pineapple juice in a 2-quart saucepan and mix well. Simmer for 10 minutes, stirring occasionally.

Combine the reserved mandarin orange juice with enough water to measure 2 cups. Add the mandarin orange juice mixture, pineapple and gelatin to the cranberry mixture. Bring to a boil, stirring constantly until the gelatin dissolves. Add the mandarin oranges and mix gently. Pour the gelatin mixture into a mold. Chill, covered, for 6 hours or until set. Invert onto a serving platter and garnish with fresh mint.

Serves 6 to 8

* *

Strawberry and Spinach Salad

SESAME POPPY DRESSING

1/2 cup salad oil

1/2 cup sugar

1/4 cup raspberry vinegar

2 tablespoons sesame seeds

1 tablespoon poppy seeds

1/4 teaspoon paprika

FOR THE DRESSING, combine the salad oil, sugar, raspberry vinegar, sesame seeds, poppy seeds and paprika in a jar with a tight-fitting lid and seal tightly. Shake to mix.

FOR THE SALAD, combine the spinach and strawberries in a salad bowl. Add the dressing and toss to coat.

Serves 4 to 6

SALAD

1 (12-ounce) package fresh spinach, torn into bite-size pieces

1 quart fresh strawberries, sliced

Watergate Salad

1 (4-ounce) package
pistachio instant
pudding mix

1 (20-ounce) can crushed
pineapple, drained
1 cup miniature marshmallows

1 cup chopped nuts
16 ounces whipped topping

Combine the pudding mix, pineapple, marshmallows and nuts in a bowl and mix well. Fold in the whipped topping. Chill, covered, until serving time.

Serves 6 to 8

* *

Antipasto Salad with Vinaigrette Dressing

VINAIGRETTE

6 tablespoons olive oil

2 1/2 tablespoons red wine
vinegar

2 tablespoons chili sauce

1 tablespoon freshly grated
Parmesan cheese

1 garlic clove, minced

1 1/2 teaspoons
Worcestershire sauce

1 1/2 teaspoons chopped
fresh parsley

1 teaspoon Italian
seasoning

1/2 teaspoon sugar

1/2 teaspoon salt

1/2 teaspoon pepper

FOR THE VINAIGRETTE, combine the olive oil, wine vinegar, chili sauce, cheese, garlic, Worcestershire sauce, parsley, Italian seasoning, sugar, salt and pepper in a jar with a tight-fitting lid and seal tightly. Shake to mix.

FOR THE SALAD, combine the lettuce, tomatoes, provolone cheese, artichokes, olives, pepperoni, beans and mushrooms in a salad bowl and mix gently. Add the vinaigrette and toss to coat. Sprinkle with the Parmesan cheese.

Serves 12

SALAD

1 head lettuce, torn into
bite-size pieces

3 Roma tomatoes,
chopped

8 ounces provolone cheese,
cut into 1/2-inch cubes

1 1/2 cups coarsely
chopped artichoke
hearts

1 (6-ounce) can pitted
black olives, drained

1 package sliced
pepperoni

1/2 cup drained garbanzo
beans

6 mushrooms, sliced

1/2 cup freshly grated
Parmesan cheese

Tossed Avocado Salad

2 lemons
3/4 cup vegetable oil
1 teaspoon Beau Monde
  seasoning

1/4 teaspoon MSG
2 avocados, sliced
6 green onions, chopped

2 heads romaine, torn into
  bite-size pieces
1 to 1 1/2 cups freshly grated
  Parmesan cheese

Squeeze the juice from the lemons into a salad bowl. Stir in the oil, Beau Monde seasoning and MSG. Add the avocados and greens onions to the lemon juice mixture and toss gently to coat.

Layer the lettuce and cheese over the avocado mixture. Chill, covered with plastic wrap, in the refrigerator. Toss just before serving.

Serves 12

* *

Broccoli Raisin Salad

Florets of 1 bunch broccoli
1 pound sliced bacon, crisp-
  cooked, crumbled
1/2 cup chopped red onion

1/2 cup chopped celery
1/3 cup sunflower seed
  kernels
1/4 cup raisins

3/4 cup sugar
1/2 cup mayonnaise
1 tablespoon vinegar

Toss the broccoli, bacon, onion, celery, sunflower seed kernels and raisins in a bowl. Fold in a mixture of the sugar, mayonnaise and vinegar. Chill well before serving.

Serves 4 to 6

Caesar Salad à la Tozzi

1 garlic clove, crushed
2 heads romaine,
    torn into bite-size
    pieces
5 garlic cloves, crushed
1¹/2 tablespoons anchovy
    paste

1 teaspoon Dijon mustard
2 eggs
1¹/2 cups grated Parmesan
    cheese
2 to 3 tablespoons
    Worcestershire sauce
Juice of 2¹/2 lemons

6 tablespoons olive oil
6 tablespoons vegetable oil
Salt and pepper to taste
Croutons
Freshly grated Parmesan
    cheese to taste

Rub 1 crushed garlic clove over the inner surface of a wooden salad bowl. Place the lettuce in the salad bowl. Chill, covered, in the refrigerator. Combine 5 crushed garlic cloves, anchovy paste and Dijon mustard in a bowl and mix well. Add the eggs and whisk until blended. Stir in 1¹/2 cups Parmesan cheese, Worcestershire sauce and lemon juice; mixture will thicken. Chill, covered, until serving time.

To serve, whisk the olive oil and vegetable oil into the anchovy mixture. Season with salt and pepper. Fold the dressing into the lettuce; do not toss until all the lettuce is evenly coated. Sprinkle with the croutons and freshly grated Parmesan cheese to taste. Serve immediately.

Serves 6 to 8

Contributed by Rick Tozzi

* *

Crunchy Tossed Salad

RED WINE DRESSING
1/4 cup olive oil
1/4 cup vegetable oil
1/4 cup sugar
2 tablespoons red wine
    vinegar
1/4 teaspoon pepper
1/4 teaspoon salt

FOR THE DRESSING, combine all the ingredients in a jar with a tight-fitting lid and seal tightly. Shake to mix. Chill for 1 hour or longer.

FOR THE SALAD, combine the iceberg lettuce, leaf lettuce, bacon, chow mein noodles, almonds and sesame seeds in a salad bowl and mix well. Add the dressing and toss to coat.

Serves 6 to 8

SALAD
1/2 head iceberg lettuce,
    torn into bite-size pieces
1/2 head leaf lettuce, torn
    into bite-size pieces
6 slices bacon,
    crisp-cooked, crumbled
3/4 cup chow mein noodles
1/3 cup almonds, toasted
1/4 cup sesame seeds, toasted

Jackson Salad

ONION DRESSING

1 cup vegetable oil

1/4 onion, minced

1 tablespoon vinegar

2 teaspoons dry mustard

1/2 teaspoon sugar

1/2 teaspoon salt

1/4 teaspoon pepper

For the dressing, combine the oil, onion, vinegar, dry mustard, sugar, salt and pepper in a blender, food processor or jar with a tight-fitting lid. Process or shake until mixed.

For the salad, toss the lettuce, hearts of palm, artichokes, bacon and bleu cheese in a salad bowl. Add the dressing just before serving and toss to coat.

Serves 10 to 12

SALAD

2 heads romaine, torn into bite-size pieces

1 (14-ounce) can hearts of palm, drained, sliced

1 (14-ounce) can artichoke hearts, drained, coarsely chopped

8 ounces sliced bacon, crisp-cooked, crumbled

4 ounces bleu cheese, crumbled, or freshly grated Parmesan cheese

* * * * * * * * * * * * * * * * * * *

Cabbage and Onion Slaw

SLAW

1 large head cabbage, shredded

1 large red onion, thinly sliced

3/4 cup sugar

For the slaw, toss the cabbage, onion and sugar in a heatproof bowl.

For the dressing, combine the vinegar, oil, salt, mustard seeds, sugar and celery salt in a medium saucepan and mix well. Cook over medium heat until the sugar dissolves and the mixture just begins to boil, stirring frequently. Remove from heat. Pour the dressing over the cabbage mixture and toss to coat. Chill, covered, for 2 hours or longer. The flavor is enhanced if the slaw is allowed to chill overnight.

Serves 8 to 10

MUSTARD DRESSING

1 cup vinegar

3/4 cup vegetable oil

1 1/2 teaspoons salt

1 teaspoon mustard seeds

1 teaspoon sugar

1 teaspoon celery salt

Fiesta Corn Bread Salad

1 (9-ounce) package corn
    bread mix
1 cup mayonnaise
1 cup sour cream
1 envelope ranch salad
    dressing mix
2 medium tomatoes, chopped

1 green bell pepper, chopped
1 bunch green onions,
    chopped
2 (16-ounce) cans pinto
    beans with jalapeño
    chiles, drained

2 cups shredded Cheddar
    cheese
2 (11-ounce) cans Mexican
    corn, drained

Prepare and bake the corn bread using package directions. Let stand until cool. Combine the mayonnaise, sour cream and dressing mix in a bowl and mix well. Toss the tomatoes, bell pepper and green onions in a bowl.

    Crumble half the corn bread into a large salad bowl. Layer with 1 can of the pinto beans, half the tomato mixture, 1 cup of the cheese and 1 can of the corn. Spread with half the mayonnaise mixture. Repeat the layers with the remaining ingredients. Chill, covered, for 2 hours.

    Serves 12 to 15

* * * * * * * * * * * * * * * * * * *

Oriental Salad

SALAD
1 (3-ounce) package any
    flavor ramen noodles
    with seasoning packet
1 (16-ounce) package
    coleslaw mix
1 (3-ounce) package salted
    sunflower seed kernels
1 (2-ounce) package
    slivered almonds

FOR THE SALAD, break the ramen noodles into a salad bowl, reserving the seasoning packet for the dressing. Add the coleslaw mix, sunflower seed kernels and almonds to the salad bowl and toss to mix.

    FOR THE DRESSING, combine the oil, sugar, vinegar and reserved seasoning in a jar with a tight-fitting lid and seal tightly. Shake to mix. Add the dressing to the slaw mixture just before serving and toss to mix.

    Serves 4 to 6

DRESSING
1/2 cup vegetable oil
3 tablespoons sugar
3 tablespoons vinegar

Mixed Green Salad with Warm Portobello Balsamic Vinaigrette

SALAD

1 pound mixed young
    salad greens
6 tablespoons crumbled
    Gorgonzola cheese
    or bleu cheese
6 tablespoons pine nuts

PORTOBELLO BALSAMIC VINAIGRETTE

2 large portobello
    mushrooms
5 tablespoons olive oil
1 garlic clove, crushed
2 tablespoons flour
1 1/2 cups Swanson's
    onion-seasoned
    beef broth
1/4 teaspoon salt
1/8 teaspoon pepper
1/2 cup balsamic vinegar

F OR THE SALAD, divide the greens equally among 4 salad plates. Sprinkle each with 1 1/2 tablespoons of the cheese and 1 1/2 tablespoons of the pine nuts. Chill, covered with plastic wrap, until serving time.

FOR THE VINAIGRETTE, rinse the mushrooms with cool water. Cut each mushroom into halves. Cut each half into 1/4-inch slices. Sauté the mushrooms in 1 tablespoon of the olive oil in a skillet until tender. Transfer the mushrooms and juices to a bowl.

Add the remaining 4 tablespoons olive oil and garlic to the skillet. Sauté over medium heat until the garlic is tender. Add the flour and mix well. Cook until smooth and bubbly. Add the broth gradually, whisking constantly until blended. Cook over medium heat for 4 minutes or until slightly thickened, stirring frequently. Stir in the salt and pepper. Add the balsamic vinegar and mix well.

Simmer for 20 minutes or until reduced by half, stirring occasionally. Stir in the undrained mushrooms. Remove from heat. Let stand until warm. If the dressing is too hot it will wilt the greens and melt the cheese. Ladle the warm dressing over the salad greens. Serve immediately.

Serves 4

Fantastic Potato Salad

6 medium potatoes
12 green onions with tops,
    trimmed, chopped
4 hard-cooked eggs, chopped
1 cup thinly sliced or
    chopped celery
1 cup chopped dill pickles

1 cup sliced black olives
12 slices bacon, crisp-
    cooked, crumbled
    (optional)
1 (2-ounce) jar chopped
    pimentos, drained
    (optional)

1 1/2 cups mayonnaise
1 tablespoon horseradish
2 teaspoons Dijon mustard
Salt and pepper to taste

Combine the potatoes with enough water to cover in a saucepan. Bring to a boil. Boil until tender but not mushy. Cool slightly. Peel the potatoes if desired and coarsely chop.

Combine the green onions, eggs, celery, dill pickles, olives, bacon and pimentos in a bowl and mix well. Add the mayonnaise, horseradish and Dijon mustard and mix gently. Fold in the potatoes. Season with salt and pepper. Garnish with celery leaves and paprika. Store, covered, in the refrigerator until serving time.

Serves 10 to 12

* * * * * * * * * * * * * * * * * * *

Enid's largest event is the annual Tri-State Music Festival, which attracts bands and musicians from all over the Southwest. Around May 1st each year, thousands of young people and their families pour into Enid to compete in marching contests, solo and ensemble contests, and a group concert along the parade route.

Started at Phillips University in the spring of 1932, the festival became known as the "Million Dollar Parade" by 1950 because of the value of the instruments that students used as they marched in the parade.

By 1977, as many as 22,000 participants marched through the streets in a single parade. Now officially called the Tri-State Music Festival, it remains the largest band festival in the nation.

French Red Potato Salad with Balsamic Herb Dressing

BALSAMIC HERB
DRESSING

1 cup extra-virgin olive oil

1/2 cup balsamic vinegar

2 garlic cloves, crushed

1 teaspoon salt

1 teaspoon sugar

1/2 teaspoon pepper

1/3 cup fresh oregano
leaves, or
2 tablespoons
dried oregano

1/3 cup coarse mustard

1/4 cup chopped fresh
parsley·

2 tablespoons fresh thyme
leaves, or 1 teaspoon
dried thyme

1 tablespoon fresh
rosemary, or
1/2 teaspoon dried
rosemary

FOR THE DRESSING, combine the olive oil, balsamic vinegar, garlic, salt, sugar and pepper in a blender container. Process at high speed for 30 to 45 seconds or until slightly frothy. Add the oregano, mustard, parsley, thyme and rosemary one at a time, pulsing between each addition until the herbs are minced. If you use dried herbs, add 2 tablespoons of water to help with the reconstitution.

FOR THE SALAD, steam the potatoes in a steamer until tender. Chill in the refrigerator. Steam the green beans in a steamer for 2 to 4 minutes or until tender-crisp. Plunge the green beans immediately into ice water to stop the cooking process. Drain and place in a bowl. Chill, covered, in the refrigerator. Cut the tomatoes vertically into halves and chill, covered. Slice the onion thinly and separate into rings. Combine the water and sugar in a bowl. Add the onion rings. Chill, covered, in the refrigerator.

SALAD

5 pounds small new red
potatoes

1 1/2 to 2 pounds fresh
green beans, trimmed

2 pints grape tomatoes

1/2 large purple onion

1 cup water

1/4 cup sugar

2 (14-ounce) cans
quartered artichoke
hearts, drained, chilled

2 (6-ounce) cans pitted
medium black olives,
drained, chilled

Cut the potatoes into halves or quarters and arrange in the center of a large serving platter or large shallow bowl. Arrange the green beans around the outer edge of the platter. Place the tomatoes and artichokes on top of the potatoes. Top with the olives and drained onion rings. Drizzle with the dressing.

Serves 20 to 25

Contributed by Sherrel Jones

Cool Cucumber Salad

DRESSING

1 1/2 cups sugar

1 cup water

3/4 cup cider vinegar

1 tablespoon salad oil

1 tablespoon prepared mustard

2 teaspoons pepper

1 teaspoon salt

1 teaspoon parsley flakes

1 teaspoon MSG

1/2 teaspoon garlic powder

FOR THE DRESSING, combine the sugar, water, vinegar, salad oil, prepared mustard, pepper, salt, parsley flakes, MSG and garlic powder in a bowl and mix well.

FOR THE SALAD, toss the cucumbers, onion and pasta in a bowl. Add the dressing and mix well. Chill, covered, to allow the flavors to blend before serving.

Serves 4 to 6

SALAD

1 or 2 large cucumbers, peeled, thinly sliced

1 medium onion, thinly sliced

12 ounces pasta (medium shells), cooked, drained

* *

Sweet-and-Sour Macaroni Salad

SWEET-AND-SOUR DRESSING

1 1/2 cups sugar

3/4 cup vinegar

1 teaspoon MSG

1 teaspoon parsley flakes

1 teaspoon garlic powder

Salt and pepper to taste

FOR THE DRESSING, combine the sugar, vinegar, MSG, parsley flakes, garlic powder, salt and pepper in a jar with a tight-fitting lid and shake to mix.

FOR THE SALAD, combine the pasta, onion, cucumber, bell pepper and pimentos in a bowl and mix well. Add the dressing and toss to coat. Chill, covered, for 8 to 10 hours.

Serves 8 to 10

SALAD

16 ounces curly macaroni, cooked, drained, rinsed

1 small onion, chopped

1 small cucumber, chopped

1 small green bell pepper, chopped

1 (2-ounce) jar chopped pimentos, drained

Wild Rice Salad

SOY DRESSING

1/3 cup vegetable oil

2 tablespoons vinegar

2 tablespoons soy sauce

1 teaspoon sugar

1/4 teaspoon pepper

FOR THE DRESSING, combine the oil, vinegar, soy sauce, sugar and pepper in a jar with a tight-fitting lid and seal tightly. Shake to mix.

FOR THE SALAD, squeeze the excess moisture from the spinach. Combine the spinach, wild rice, white rice, almonds, green onions and bacon in a salad bowl and mix well. Add the dressing and toss to coat.

Serves 6 to 8

SALAD

1 (10-ounce) package frozen chopped spinach, thawed, drained

3 cups cooked wild rice

1 1/2 cups cooked white rice

1/2 cup slivered almonds, toasted

1/4 cup sliced green onions

4 slices bacon, crisp-cooked, crumbled

* * * * * * * * * * * * * * * * * * *

Mango Chutney Chicken Salad

3 boneless skinless chicken breasts

3/4 cup sour cream or reduced-fat sour cream

3/4 cup mayonnaise or reduced-fat mayonnaise

1/2 cup chopped celery

1/2 cup chopped pecans

1/3 cup mango chutney

3 green onions, sliced

1 teaspoon salt

1/2 teaspoon pepper

1/2 teaspoon curry powder (optional)

1/2 teaspoon dry mustard

Grated lemon zest to taste

Lettuce leaves

Bake, poach or grill the chicken until cooked through. Cool slightly and cut into bite-size pieces. Combine the chicken, sour cream, mayonnaise, celery, pecans, chutney and green onions in a bowl and mix well. Stir in the salt, pepper, curry powder, dry mustard and lemon zest. Chill, covered, until serving time. Spoon the chicken salad onto a lettuce-lined serving platter, into pita pockets or spread on croissants or your favorite sandwich bread.

For variety, add one 8-ounce can drained water chestnuts, sliced red grapes and/or sliced mangoes or substitute 1/2 cup toasted slivered almonds for the pecans.

Serves 6 to 8

Chicken and Black Bean Salad

LIME VINAIGRETTE

2/3 cup olive oil

1/4 cup fresh lime juice

1/4 cup minced fresh
   parsley

1 tablespoon sugar

2 garlic cloves, minced

1 teaspoon chili powder

1 teaspoon salt

1/2 teaspoon pepper

*F*OR THE VINAIGRETTE, combine the olive oil, lime juice, parsley, sugar, garlic, chili powder, salt and pepper in a jar with a tight-fitting lid and seal tightly. Shake to mix.

FOR THE SALAD, combine the beans, corn, bell pepper, green onions, green chiles, jalapeño chile and jalapeño juice in a bowl and mix gently. Add 2 tablespoons of the vinaigrette to the bean mixture and toss to coat. Set aside.

Pound the chicken between sheets of waxed paper with a meat mallet to flatten. Pour the salad dressing over the chicken in a shallow dish, turning to coat. Marinate, covered, in the refrigerator for 1 to 24 hours, turning occasionally. Grill the chicken over medium-hot coals for 5 minutes per side or until cooked through. Cut into diagonal slices.

TO ASSEMBLE, divide the salad greens equally among 6 serving plates. Top with the bean mixture and sliced chicken. Drizzle with the remaining vinaigrette. May be prepared in advance, chilled and served cold.

Serves 6

SALAD

1 (15-ounce) can black
   beans, drained, rinsed

1 (11-ounce) can corn,
   drained

1 small red bell pepper,
   julienned

1/3 cup sliced green
   onions

2 tablespoons chopped
   green chiles

1 teaspoon finely
   chopped pickled
   jalapeño chile

1 teaspoon jalapeño
   juice (from jar)

4 boneless skinless
   chicken breasts

1/2 cup Italian salad
   dressing

10 cups mixed salad
   greens, torn

Luncheon Chicken Salad

PINEAPPLE DRESSING

1 (20-ounce) can
pineapple chunks

1/3 cup vinegar

1/4 cup packed brown
sugar

2 tablespoons vegetable
oil

1 tablespoon soy sauce

F OR THE DRESSING, drain the pineapple, reserving 1/2 cup of the juice for the dressing and the pineapple for the salad. Combine the reserved pineapple juice, vinegar, brown sugar, oil and soy sauce in a jar with a tight-fitting lid and seal tightly. Shake to mix.

FOR THE SALAD, cook the pasta using package directions until of the desired degree of doneness. Drain, rinse with cold water and drain. Spread the almonds in a single layer on a baking sheet. Toast at 375 degrees for 5 to

SALAD

1 cup orzo

1/2 cup slivered almonds

1 (11-ounce) can mandarin
oranges, drained

3 cups chopped cooked
chicken

2 cups seedless red grape
halves

1 cup chopped celery

1/4 cup chopped onion

10 minutes or until light golden brown, stirring occasionally, or spread the almonds on a microwave-safe plate. Microwave on High for 3 to 4 minutes or until golden brown, stirring frequently.

Combine the reserved pineapple, pasta, mandarin oranges, chicken, grapes, celery and onion in a bowl and mix well. Add the dressing and toss to coat. Chill, covered, until serving time. Sprinkle with the almonds just before serving.

Makes 8 (1 1/2-cup) servings

* *

Everyday Vinaigrette

Combine 2/3 cup corn oil or canola oil, 1/3 cup vinegar, 1/4 cup sugar, 1 tablespoon minced onion, 1 teaspoon dry mustard and 1 teaspoon salt in a jar with a tight-fitting lid and shake to mix. Chill in the refrigerator. Drizzle the chilled vinaigrette over a mixture of red leaf lettuce, sliced mushrooms, mandarin oranges, grape halves, sliced red onions, toasted almonds and grated Parmesan cheese or the salad of your choice.

Shrimp Salad

2 cups mayonnaise

1/4 cup cooked fresh
   spinach, finely chopped,
   drained

1 hard-cooked egg, chopped

2 shallots, finely chopped

4 garlic cloves, finely
   chopped

1 tablespoon Worcestershire
   sauce

1 tablespoon Creole mustard

1 tablespoon fresh lemon
   juice

1/3 ounce anchovy paste

1/8 teaspoon liquid hot
   red pepper sauce

1 1/2 pounds deveined
   peeled cooked shrimp

1 cup mayonnaise

3/4 cup chopped celery

Juice of 1/2 lemon

Salt to taste

Combine 2 cups mayonnaise, spinach, egg, shallots, garlic, Worcestershire sauce, Creole mustard, 1 tablespoon lemon juice, anchovy paste and red pepper sauce in a bowl and mix well.

Combine the shrimp, 1 cup mayonnaise, celery, juice of 1/2 lemon and salt in a bowl and mix gently. Stir in the sauce.

Serves 6

* * * * * * * * * * * * * * * * * *

Simple Coleslaw Dressing

Add your favorite ingredients to this everyday starter recipe. Mix 3/4 cup mayonnaise, 2 tablespoons sugar, 3/4 teaspoon salt, 1/4 to 1/2 teaspoon garlic powder and 1/4 teaspoon pepper. Chill, covered, in the refrigerator.

Banana Poppy Seed Dressing

1 ripe banana
1 cup sour cream
1/4 cup sugar

1 tablespoon poppy seeds
1 tablespoon lemon juice

1 teaspoon dry mustard
3/4 teaspoon salt

Mash the banana in a bowl. Stir in the sour cream, sugar, poppy seeds, lemon juice, dry mustard and salt. Chill, covered, in the refrigerator. Serve over fruit salads or over orange or grapefruit sections. Use the same day of preparation for optimal flavor.

  Makes 1 3/4 cups

* *

Roasted Garlic Dressing

15 to 20 peeled garlic cloves
2 tablespoons olive oil
2 tablespoons extra-virgin
  olive oil
1 tablespoon fresh lemon
  juice

1 tablespoon white wine
  vinegar
1 teaspoon Dijon mustard
1 teaspoon fresh thyme
  leaves

1 teaspoon minced fresh
  rosemary
Salt and freshly ground
  pepper to taste
6 tablespoons extra-virgin
  olive oil

Arrange the garlic cloves in a ramekin and drizzle with 2 tablespoons olive oil. Place the ramekin on a baking sheet. Roast, covered with foil, at 400 degrees for 1 hour. Let stand until cool.

  Combine the roasted garlic, 2 tablespoons extra-virgin olive oil, lemon juice, wine vinegar, Dijon mustard, thyme, rosemary, salt and pepper in a food processor or blender container. Process until puréed, adding 6 tablespoons extra-virgin olive oil gradually during the process. Taste and adjust the seasonings. Use immediately or chill, covered, in the refrigerator.

  Makes 1 cup

Ingredient Equivalents

Food	Amount Before Preparation	Approximate Measure After Preparation
Grains		
Macaroni	1 cup (3$1/2$ ounces)	2$1/2$ cups cooked
Noodles, medium	3 cups (4 ounces)	3 cups cooked
Spaghetti	8 ounces	4 cups cooked
Long grain rice	1 cup (7 ounces)	3 cups cooked
Quick-cooking rice	1 cup (3 ounces)	2 cups cooked
Popcorn	$1/3$ to $1/2$ cup	8 cups popped
Crumbs		
Bread	1 slice	3/4 cup soft crumbs or $1/4$ cup fine dry crumbs
Saltine crackers	14 crackers	$1/2$ cup finely crushed
Rich round crackers	12 crackers	$1/2$ cup finely crushed
Graham crackers	7 squares	$1/2$ cup finely crushed
Gingersnaps	7 cookies	$1/2$ cup finely crushed
Vanilla wafers	11 cookies	$1/2$ cup finely crushed
Fruits		
Apples	1 medium	1 cup sliced
Bananas	1 medium	$1/3$ cup mashed
Lemons	1 medium	3 tablespoons juice; 2 teaspoons shredded peel
Limes	1 medium	2 tablespoons juice; 1$1/2$ teaspoons shredded peel
Oranges	1 medium	$1/4$ to $1/3$ cup juice; 4 teaspoons shredded peel
Peaches, pears	1 medium	$1/2$ cup sliced
Rhubarb	1 pound	2 cups cooked
Strawberries	4 cups whole	4 cups sliced
Vegetables		
Cabbage	1 pound (1 small)	5 cups shredded
Carrots, without tops	1 pound (6 to 8 medium)	3 cups shredded or 2$1/4$ cups chopped
Cauliflower	1 medium head	4$1/2$ cups sliced
Celery	1 stalk	$1/2$ cup chopped
Green beans	1 pound (4 cups)	2$1/2$ cups cooked
Green bell peppers	1 large	1 cup chopped
Lettuce	1 medium head	6 cups torn
Mushrooms	$1/2$ pound (3 cups)	1 cup cooked
Onions	1 medium	$1/2$ cup chopped
Potatoes	3 medium	2 cups cubed or 1$1/4$ cups mashed
Spinach	1 pound	12 cups torn
Tomatoes	1 medium	$1/2$ cup chopped
Miscellaneous		
Cheese	4 ounces	1 cup shredded
Whipping cream	1 cup	2 cups whipped
Ground beef	1 pound raw	2$3/4$ cups cooked
Cooked meat	1 pound	3 cups chopped
Chicken breasts	1$1/2$ pounds (2 whole medium)	2 cups chopped cooked chicken

Main Dishes

Two-Step Tenderloin

TENDERLOIN

2 tablespoons Dijon
    mustard

1 tablespoon olive oil

1 (4-pound) beef tenderloin,
    trimmed

1 tablespoon freshly ground
    pepper

1 tablespoon oregano,
    crushed

1 tablespoon thyme,
    crushed

1 tablespoon finely snipped
    chives

2 garlic cloves, minced

1 teaspoon salt

FOR THE TENDERLOIN, combine the Dijon mustard and olive oil in a small bowl and mix well. Brush the mustard mixture over the entire surface of the tenderloin. Combine the pepper, oregano, thyme, chives, garlic and salt in a bowl and mix well. Pat the seasoning mixture on all sides of the tenderloin.

Arrange the tenderloin on a rack in a large shallow roasting pan. Let stand at room temperature for 30 minutes. Bake at 425 degrees for 45 minutes or until a meat thermometer registers 140 degrees for rare. Remove from oven. Let stand for 45 minutes. Chill, wrapped, in the refrigerator.

FOR THE SAUCE, combine the mayonnaise, sour cream, Dijon mustard, wine vinegar, chives and Worcestershire sauce in a bowl and mix well. Chill, covered, in the refrigerator.

TO SERVE, bring the tenderloin to room temperature and slice as desired. Serve with the sauce.

Serves 12

MUSTARD SAUCE

1/2 cup mayonnaise

1/2 cup sour cream

1/4 cup Dijon mustard

1 tablespoon white wine
    vinegar

1 tablespoon snipped
    chives

1 teaspoon Worcestershire
    sauce

Beef Tenderloin with Coffee Crust

1 (4-pound) beef tenderloin
1/2 cup red wine vinegar
1/2 cup soy sauce
1/2 cup chopped onion

1/3 cup vegetable oil
1/4 cup packed brown sugar
1/4 cup ketchup
1 teaspoon salt

1 teaspoon pepper
2 tablespoons peppercorns
1/4 cup coffee beans

Place the tenderloin in a shallow dish. Combine the wine vinegar, soy sauce, onion, oil, brown sugar, ketchup, salt and pepper in a bowl and mix well. Pour over the tenderloin, turning to coat. Marinate, covered, in the refrigerator for 2 to 12 hours, turning occasionally; drain.

Grind the peppercorns and coffee beans in a food processor. Rub the peppercorn mixture over the entire surface of the tenderloin. Grill the tenderloin over hot coals or roast at 450 degrees for approximately 15 minutes per pound. Let rest for 15 minutes before slicing. When purchasing tenderloin, allow 8 ounces per guest.

Serves 8

* * * * * * * * * * * * * * * * * * *

The Sucker Convention, April 1, 1905

On April 1, 1905, the local jailer made an urgent call to attorney Charles West, who one day would be the Attorney General for the State of Oklahoma. He told West there was a dying young man at the jail who desperately needed to write a will.

Upon entering the jail through locked doors, West came upon a "dead soldier," an empty beer bottle lying on the floor. "April Fool!" shouted the jailer. West thought it was a great joke and began calling all his friends.

By the end of the day, one by one, other attorneys, doctors, and leading businessmen were led into the jail, where they got a derisive "April Fool, Sucker!" shouted at them by the assembled masses. This day became known as "The Sucker Convention."

Spicy Enchiladas

1 (2- to 3-pound) chuck roast
1 (16-ounce) can chopped
   tomatoes
1/4 cup hot salsa
1/4 cup water
5 garlic cloves, minced
2 1/2 tablespoons chili
   powder
2 tablespoons oregano

1 1/2 teaspoons cumin
Salt and pepper to taste
12 flour tortillas
1 small onion, chopped
Chopped jalapeño chiles
   (optional)
Chopped green chiles
1 (10-ounce) can enchilada
   sauce

1 (8-ounce) can tomato
   sauce
Shredded Cheddar and
   Monterey Jack cheese to
   taste
Chopped fresh cilantro
   (optional)

Place the roast in a baking pan. Combine the undrained tomatoes, salsa, water, garlic, chili powder, oregano, cumin, salt and pepper in a bowl and mix well. Pour the tomato mixture over the roast. Bake, tightly covered, at 300 degrees for 3 hours. Remove the roast from the oven and shred. May be prepared 1 day in advance and stored, covered, in the refrigerator.

Dip the tortillas in hot water for 1 second and pat dry with paper towels. Spoon some of the beef, onion, jalapeño chiles and green chiles onto the center of each tortilla. Roll to enclose the filling. Arrange seam side down in a greased 10×15-inch baking dish.

Mix the enchilada sauce and tomato sauce in a bowl. Pour over the top of the enchiladas. Sprinkle with cheese. Bake, covered tightly, at 350 degrees for 25 minutes. Remove cover and sprinkle with more cheese. Bake for 10 minutes longer. Sprinkle with cilantro.

Makes 12 enchiladas

Fajita-Style Shredded Beef

Place one 3- to 5-pound beef roast in a slow cooker. Pour 1 large jar of medium picante sauce over the roast. Cook, covered, on Low for 6 to 8 hours or until the beef is cooked through; shred. Top heated flour tortillas with shredded beef and sour cream. Roll to enclose the filling.

Mom's Roast Beef

1 tablespoon vegetable oil
1 (2 1/2-pound) eye of round
  beef roast
1 medium onion, chopped
1 cup brewed coffee

3/4 cup water
1 beef bouillon cube
2 teaspoons basil
1 teaspoon rosemary
1 teaspoon salt

1 garlic clove, minced
1/2 teaspoon pepper
1/4 cup flour
1/4 cup water

Heat the oil in a Dutch oven. Brown the roast on all sides in the hot oil. Stir in the onion. Cook until tender. Add the coffee, 3/4 cup water, bouillon cube, basil, rosemary, salt, garlic and pepper and mix well.

Simmer, covered, for 2 1/2 hours or until the roast is of the desired degree of doneness. Combine the flour and 1/4 cup water in a small bowl and mix until smooth. Stir the flour mixture into the pan drippings. Cook until thickened, stirring constantly. Remove the roast to a serving platter and slice. Ladle the gravy into a gravy boat and serve with the roast.

Serves 8

* *

Drip Beef

1 (4- to 5-pound) beef roast
2 (14-ounce) cans beef broth
1 tablespoon salt

1 tablespoon pepper
1 tablespoon basil
1 tablespoon garlic powder

1 tablespoon rosemary
1 tablespoon oregano
2 or 3 bay leaves

Brown the roast on all sides in a skillet. Transfer the roast to a slow cooker. Add the broth, salt, pepper, basil, garlic powder, rosemary, oregano and bay leaves to the slow cooker. Add enough water to cover the roast.

Cook, covered, on Low for 8 to 10 hours. Discard the bay leaves. Remove the roast to a platter and shred if needed. Serve the shredded beef on buns with pan juices for dipping. Rump roast is preferred for this recipe.

Serves 10 to 12

Southern Chicken-Fried Steak with Spicy Gravy

CHICKEN-FRIED STEAK

1 1/2 pounds cube, bottom
    round or rump steaks
1/4 cup milk
1 egg
1 cup flour
2 teaspoons black pepper
1 1/2 teaspoons salt
3/4 teaspoon (or more)
    ground red pepper
1/4 cup shortening

FOR THE STEAK, rinse the cube steaks with cool water and pat dry. Pound the steaks between sheets of waxed paper with a meat mallet to flatten. Whisk the milk and egg in a bowl. Combine the flour, black pepper, salt and red pepper in a shallow dish and mix well.

Dip each steak in the egg mixture and then coat with the flour mixture. Let stand for 10 minutes. Heat the shortening in a large skillet until it sizzles when a drop of water is added. Fry the steaks in the hot shortening for 3 minutes per side or until golden brown, turning once. Drain, reserving 2 to 3 tablespoons of the pan drippings for the gravy. Place the steaks on a platter and cover to keep warm.

FOR THE GRAVY, sauté the onion in the reserved pan drippings in a skillet for 2 to 3 minutes. Add the flour and mix well. Cook until bubbly, stirring constantly. Stir in the milk. Cook until thickened, stirring constantly. Serve the gravy with the steaks.

Serves 4

SPICY GRAVY

1 small onion, thinly sliced
2 to 3 tablespoons flour
1 cup milk

* * * * * * * * * * * * * * * * * * * *

Good Gravy!

★ *Browned flour will give a richer flavor and color to gravy.*

★ *For clear gravy, use cornstarch or arrowroot. For opaque, use flour.*

★ *Before adding any thickener to gravy, always mix with liquid first to form a paste, or it will be lumpy.*

★ *For a good meat gravy, never add any liquids to the meat before it is browned.*

Stuffed Flank Steak

2 cups chopped fresh spinach, or 1 (10-ounce) package frozen spinach
1 cup shredded Swiss cheese
1 (6-ounce) jar marinated artichoke hearts, drained, chopped
3/4 cup finely chopped green onions
1/2 cup grated Parmesan cheese

1/2 cup soft bread crumbs (about 1 slice bread)
4 slices bacon, crisp-cooked, crumbled
1/2 cup chopped fresh mushrooms
1/4 cup minced fresh parsley
1 (1 1/2- to 2-pound) beef flank steak
2 tablespoons butter
2 garlic cloves, minced
1 teaspoon salt

1 teaspoon freshly ground pepper
2 tablespoons vegetable oil
1 (14-ounce) can beef broth
1/2 cup water
1/3 pound fresh mushrooms, sliced
1 large onion, sliced
1/2 cup minced fresh parsley
2 teaspoons cornstarch
2 tablespoons water

Thaw the spinach and drain. Squeeze to remove excess moisture. Combine the spinach, Swiss cheese, artichokes, green onions, Parmesan cheese, bread crumbs, bacon, 1/2 cup mushrooms and 1/4 cup parsley in a bowl and mix well. Place the steak in a 1-gallon sealable plastic bag. Pound the steak with a meat mallet until the steak fills the bag, approximately 10×14 inches.

Heat the butter in a small saucepan until melted. Stir in the garlic. Brush the butter mixture over 1 side of the steak. Spread the spinach mixture over the butter mixture. Roll as for a jelly roll. Tie securely with kitchen twine in 5 or 6 places. Seal the ends with wooden picks. Rub the steak roll with the salt and pepper.

Heat the oil in a large skillet. Sear the steak roll on all sides in the hot oil until brown. Place in a roasting pan. Add the broth, 1/2 cup water, 1/3 pound mushrooms, onion and 1/2 cup parsley. Bake at 300 degrees for 40 to 55 minutes or until the desired degree of doneness. Transfer the steak roll to a cutting board, reserving the pan drippings. Let rest for 5 to 10 minutes.

Cut the roll into 3/4- to 1-inch slices and arrange the slices in a pinwheel fashion on a serving platter. Combine the cornstarch and 2 teaspoons water in a small bowl and mix well. Stir the cornstarch mixture into the reserved pan drippings. Cook until thickened, stirring constantly. Serve the gravy with the sliced steak roll and mashed potatoes or serve with hot cooked noodles drizzled with Alfredo sauce. Garnish with sprigs of fresh parsley.

Serves 4 to 6

Sizzling Steak with Roasted Vegetables

STEAKS

1/3 cup dry red wine

1/4 cup beef broth

2 tablespoons balsamic
vinegar

1 tablespoon brown sugar

1/4 teaspoon pepper

3 garlic cloves, minced

4 (4-ounce) beef tenderloin
steaks, 1 inch thick

FOR THE STEAKS, combine the wine, broth, balsamic vinegar, brown sugar, pepper and garlic in a large sealable plastic bag. Add the steaks and seal tightly. Marinate in the refrigerator for 2 hours, turning occasionally.

FOR THE VEGETABLES, combine the bell peppers, potatoes, shallots, oil and salt in a 9×13-inch baking dish and toss to mix. Bake at 400 degrees for 45 minutes or until the potatoes are tender, stirring occasionally.

TO ASSEMBLE, drain the steaks reserving the marinade. Sprinkle a mixture of the pepper and salt over both sides of the steaks. Heat the oil in a large nonstick skillet over medium-high heat. Add the steaks.

Sauté for 3 minutes on each side or until the steaks are the desired degree of

ROASTED VEGETABLES

2 red bell peppers, cut into
1-inch pieces

2 yellow bell peppers, cut
into 1-inch pieces

12 small red potatoes,
cut into quarters

3 shallots, cut into halves

2 teaspoons vegetable oil

1/4 teaspoon salt

ASSEMBLY

2 teaspoons pepper

1/2 teaspoon salt

1 teaspoon vegetable oil

1 teaspoon horseradish

doneness. Remove the steaks to a serving platter and cover to keep warm, reserving the pan drippings. Stir the reserved marinade into the reserved pan drippings. Bring to a boil. Boil for 1 minute, scraping the bottom of the skillet to loosen any browned bits. Stir in the horseradish. Arrange the roasted vegetables around the steaks. Drizzle the horseradish sauce over the steaks and vegetables. Serve immediately.

Serves 4

Saucy Brisket

Garlic salt to taste

Lemon pepper to taste

Chili powder to taste

Salt and black pepper to taste

1 (5- to 6-pound) beef brisket

1/2 cup Worcestershire sauce

Sprinkle the garlic salt, lemon pepper, chili powder, salt and black pepper liberally over the surface of the brisket. Place the brisket in a roasting pan. Pour the Worcestershire sauce over the top. Add water to the fat line of the brisket.

Roast, covered, at 300 degrees for 4 to 5 hours. Remove from oven. Chill, covered, in the roasting pan for 8 to 10 hours. Skim the fat from the pan drippings, reserving the pan drippings. Trim the fat from the brisket.

Slice the brisket across the grain into thin slices. Layer the slices in a baking dish. Pour the reserved pan drippings over the brisket. Marinate, covered, in the refrigerator for 8 to 10 hours. Reheat in the oven or in the microwave just before serving.

Serves 10 to 12

* * * * * * * * * * * * * * * * * * * *

Belgian Beef

1/4 cup flour

1 1/2 teaspoons garlic
powder

1 1/2 to 2 pounds boneless
beef stew meat

2 tablespoons vegetable oil

1 (12-ounce) bottle beer

2/3 cup teriyaki baste and
glaze

2 cups coarsely chopped
potatoes

1 onion, cut into chunks

1/2 teaspoon pepper

1/2 cup chopped green
onions

Combine the flour and garlic powder in a shallow dish and mix well. Coat the beef in the flour mixture. Brown the beef on all sides in the oil in a heavy saucepan. Stir in the beer and teriyaki baste. Bring to a boil; reduce heat.

Simmer, covered, for 1 hour, stirring occasionally. Stir in the potatoes, onion and pepper. Simmer, covered, for 45 minutes or until the beef and potatoes are tender, stirring occasionally. Remove from heat. Stir in the green onions.

Serves 6

Chiles Rellenos Casserole

1 pound ground beef
1/2 cup chopped onion
1 tablespoon taco
   seasoning mix
1/2 teaspoon salt

1/4 teaspoon pepper
2 (4-ounce) cans whole
   green chiles, drained
2 cups shredded cheese
1/4 cup flour

1 1/2 cups milk
4 eggs, beaten
1/2 teaspoon salt
1/8 teaspoon pepper
Hot sauce to taste

Brown the ground beef with the onion in a skillet, stirring until the ground beef is crumbly; drain. Stir in the seasoning mix, 1/2 teaspoon salt and 1/4 teaspoon pepper. Remove from heat.

Cut the green chiles into halves and remove the seeds. Arrange half the chiles cut side up in a lightly greased 10-inch round baking dish. Sprinkle with 1 cup of the cheese. Top with the ground beef mixture. Layer with the remaining chiles cut side up and remaining 1 cup cheese.

Mix the flour and 1/4 cup of the milk in a bowl. Whisk in the eggs, remaining 1 1/4 cups milk, 1/2 teaspoon salt, 1/8 teaspoon pepper and hot sauce. Pour over the prepared layers. Bake at 350 degrees for 45 to 50 minutes or until bubbly. Let stand for 5 minutes.

Serves 6 to 8

* *

Cavitini

1 1/2 pounds ground beef
2 (15-ounce) cans tomato
   sauce
1 (2-ounce) can sliced black
   olives, drained
3 cups macaroni wheels,
   cooked, drained

1/2 (8-ounce) package sliced
   pepperoni
1 onion, chopped
1/2 green bell pepper,
   chopped
1 (4-ounce) can sliced
   mushrooms, drained

2 tablespoons sugar
1 to 2 teaspoons Italian
   seasoning
1 teaspoon salt
1 teaspoon pepper
Shredded mozzarella cheese
   to taste

Brown the ground beef in a skillet, stirring until crumbly; drain. Mix the ground beef with the next 11 ingredients in a bowl. Spoon into a baking dish. Bake at 350 degrees for 30 minutes. Sprinkle generously with mozzarella cheese. Bake for 10 minutes longer.

Serves 6

Chalupa Casserole

1/2 cup chopped onion
2 tablespoons vegetable oil
2 pounds ground beef
1 cup water

3 tablespoons chili powder
2 tablespoons flour
1 (10-ounce) can tomato
    soup

1 1/2 cups shredded cheese
1 1/2 cups light cream
Salt to taste
12 flour tortillas

Sauté the onion in the oil in a skillet until tender. Add the ground beef. Cook until the ground beef is brown and crumbly, stirring frequently; drain. Stir in the water, chili powder and flour. Cook, covered, for 15 minutes, stirring occasionally. Stir in the soup, cheese, cream and salt. Remove from heat.

Cut the tortillas into strips. Layer the tortilla strips and ground beef mixture 1/2 at a time in a greased baking dish. Bake at 325 degrees for 25 minutes or until bubbly. Serve with chips and a crisp green salad. May be prepared in advance and stored, covered, in the refrigerator. Bake just before serving.

Serves 6 to 8

* *

Meat Loaf Cordon Bleu

2 eggs
1/2 cup chicken broth
1/4 cup bread crumbs
2 garlic cloves, minced
2 tablespoons minced parsley
2 teaspoons salt

1 teaspoon tarragon
1 teaspoon dry mustard
1/4 teaspoon pepper
2 pounds lean ground beef
1/2 cup chopped green
    onions

1 tablespoon butter
1 cup shredded Swiss cheese
2 ounces chopped smoked
    ham
2 tablespoons minced parsley

Beat the eggs in a mixing bowl until blended. Add the broth, bread crumbs, garlic, 2 tablespoons parsley, salt, tarragon, dry mustard and pepper. Beat until mixed. Mix in the ground beef. Sauté the green onions in the butter in a skillet until tender. Combine the green onions, cheese, ham and 2 tablespoons parsley in a bowl.

Divide the ground beef mixture into 2 equal portions. Pat 1 portion of the ground beef mixture into a loaf pan. Top with the cheese mixture. Pat the remaining ground beef mixture over the cheese mixture.

Bake at 350 degrees for 45 minutes; drain. Bake for 30 minutes longer. Let stand in the pan for 15 minutes. Serve hot or at room temperature.

Serves 8

Veal Vitello

2 pounds thin veal cutlets
Flour
1/2 cup (1 stick) butter

3/4 cup dry white wine
Juice of 1 or 2 lemons
   (use 2 for more tartness)

2 tablespoons capers

Pound the cutlets between sheets of waxed paper with a meat mallet until approximately the size of your hand. Coat the cutlets lightly with flour. Melt the butter in a medium skillet. Fry each cutlet in the butter for 3 to 4 minutes per side or until golden brown. Remove the cutlets with a slotted spoon to paper towels to drain, reserving the pan drippings.

Add the wine and lemon juice to the reserved pan drippings and stir to loosen any browned bits. Stir in the capers. Cook until the browned bits are blended and the mixture is reduced by half, stirring constantly. Return the cutlets to the skillet. Cook just until heated through. Serve immediately with hot pasta or risotto.

Serves 6 to 8

Contributed by Rick Tozzi

* *

Veal Marsala

2 pounds veal or boneless
   skinless chicken breasts
Flour

1/2 cup (1 stick) butter
3/4 cup marsala

5 to 6 tablespoons chicken
   broth
2 green onions, chopped

Slice the veal thinly. Pound the veal between sheets of waxed paper with a meat mallet. Coat the cutlets lightly with flour. Heat the butter in a medium skillet. Fry the cutlets in the butter for 3 to 4 minutes per side or until golden brown. Drain on paper towels, reserving the pan drippings.

Add the wine, broth and green onions to the reserved pan drippings and stir to loosen any browned bits. Cook over medium heat for 5 to 7 minutes or until the mixture is reduced by half, stirring constantly. Return the cutlets to the skillet. Cook just until heated through. Serve immediately with hot pasta or risotto.

Serves 6 to 8

Contributed by Rick Tozzi

Eggplant Parmigiana Perfection

3 large eggplant,
  peeled
Salt to taste
10 to 12 eggs
1/2 cup grated Parmesan
  cheese
1/4 cup parsley flakes

1 tablespoon granulated
  garlic powder
1/4 cup milk
15 ounces Italian-style bread
  crumbs
8 to 12 ounces grated
  Parmesan cheese

1/2 cup parsley flakes
2 tablespoons granulated
  garlic powder
Vegetable oil
Olive oil
Tomato sauce
Shredded mozzarella cheese

Cut each eggplant into 1/4-inch slices. Sprinkle one side of each slice lightly with salt. Layer the slices in a colander and weight with a dinner plate. Drain for 30 to 60 minutes. Pat dry with paper towels.

Whisk the eggs in a bowl. Stir in 1/2 cup Parmesan cheese, 1/4 cup parsley flakes, 1 tablespoon garlic powder and milk. Mix the bread crumbs, 8 to 12 ounces Parmesan cheese, 1/2 cup parsley flakes and 2 tablespoons garlic powder in a bowl. If you can't smell the cheese and garlic add more!

Dip each eggplant slice in the egg mixture and coat with the bread crumb mixture. Heat an equal amount of vegetable oil and olive oil in an electric skillet at 300 to 325 degrees until hot. Fry the eggplant in the hot oil mixture until golden brown on both sides, turning once; drain.

Spread a thin layer of tomato sauce in a baking dish. Layer with some of the eggplant and mozzarella cheese. Repeat the layering process up to 3 times. Bake at 325 degrees for 15 to 20 minutes.

Serves 8

Contributed by Rick Tozzi

A full-blooded Italian from New York City, Rick Tozzi is passionate about authentic Italian cuisine. And in true Italian fashion, cooking at the Tozzi house is "a family affair." Rick's wife Brenda, son Anthony, and daughter Victoria, cook with Rick, preparing multi-course Italian meals in the kitchen he and Brenda designed. Sometimes Rick's three grown daughters and their families join in the fun as well. The Tozzis cook for friends as well as for major charity events. As Rick puts it, "My best times are spent in the kitchen!"

Italian Cheese Meat Loaf

1 pound ground beef
3/4 cup bread crumbs
1 egg, beaten

2 (8-ounce) cans tomato
    sauce
1 teaspoon salt
1/2 teaspoon oregano

1/8 teaspoon pepper
2 cups shredded mozzarella
    cheese

Mix the ground beef, bread crumbs and egg in a bowl. Blend the tomato sauce, salt, oregano and pepper in a bowl. Add 1/3 cup of the tomato sauce mixture to the ground beef mixture.

Shape the ground beef mixture into a flat rectangle on a sheet of waxed paper. Sprinkle the cheese down the middle of the rectangle. Roll up and press the ends to seal. Arrange the meat loaf seam side down in a baking pan. Bake at 350 degrees for 1 hour. Pour the remaining tomato sauce mixture over the meat loaf. Bake for 15 minutes longer.

Serves 4 to 6

* * * * * * * * * * * * * * * * * * *

Venetian Meat Pie

1 (2-crust) pie pastry
1 pound ground beef
1 small onion, chopped
1/2 cup chopped bell pepper
1 teaspoon chopped fresh
    parsley
2 tablespoons olive oil

1 teaspoon salt
1 teaspoon oregano
1/2 teaspoon garlic salt
1/2 cup Italian bread
    crumbs
1/4 cup shredded Cheddar
    cheese

1 medium zucchini, thinly
    sliced
2 tomatoes, thinly sliced
2 tablespoons olive oil
1 tablespoon (about) milk
Pepper to taste
Garlic salt to taste

Fit half the pastry into a pie plate. Brown the ground beef with the onion, bell pepper and parsley in 2 tablespoons olive oil in a skillet, stirring until the ground beef is crumbly; drain. Stir in the salt, oregano and 1/2 teaspoon garlic salt. Combine the bread crumbs and cheese in a bowl and mix well.

Layer the zucchini, ground beef mixture and bread crumb mixture 1/2 at a time in the prepared pie plate. Arrange the sliced tomatoes over the top and drizzle with 2 tablespoons olive oil. Top with the remaining pastry, sealing the edge and making vents in the top. Brush the pastry with the milk. Sprinkle lightly with pepper and garlic salt to taste. Bake at 350 degrees for 1 hour or until light brown.

Serves 6 to 8

Pork Tenderloin with Spicy Mustard Sauce

PORK TENDERLOIN

1/2 cup teriyaki sauce

1/4 cup bourbon

2 tablespoons brown sugar

4 3/4 pounds pork
tenderloin

FOR THE TENDERLOIN, combine the teriyaki sauce, bourbon and brown sugar in a 7×11-inch dish and mix well. Add the tenderloin and turn to coat. Marinate, covered, in the refrigerator for 8 to 10 hours, turning occasionally; drain.

Place the tenderloin on a rack in a shallow roasting pan. Bake at 400 degrees for 30 minutes or until a meat thermometer registers 160 degrees for medium. Let rest for 5 to 10 minutes.

FOR THE SAUCE, combine the mayonnaise, dry mustard, vinegar and teriyaki sauce in a bowl and mix well. Chill, covered, in the refrigerator. Sprinkle with paprika just before serving.

SPICY MUSTARD SAUCE

2/3 cup mayonnaise or
mayonnaise-type salad
dressing

2 to 3 teaspoons dry
mustard

2 teaspoons white vinegar

2 teaspoons teriyaki sauce

Paprika

PARTY ROLLS

1 1/2 (25-ounce) packages
frozen roll dough

FOR THE ROLLS, thaw 3 dozen dough balls using package directions. Cut each ball into halves with kitchen shears. Roll each portion into a ball and arrange on lightly greased baking sheets. Spray the dough balls lightly with nonstick cooking spray.

Let rise, covered, in a warm place free from drafts for 40 minutes or until doubled in bulk. Bake at 350 degrees for 10 to 12 minutes or until golden brown. Remove the rolls to a wire rack to cool. Cut each roll to but not through the bottom into halves with a serrated knife. You may store in heavy-duty sealable plastic bags for up to 2 days.

TO SERVE, cut the tenderloin into thin slices on a cutting board. Serve the sliced tenderloin with the rolls and sauce.

Serves 12 to 15

Pork and Pasta with Bacon Balsamic Vinaigrette

Salt and pepper to taste
1 pork tenderloin
1 tablespoon olive oil
1/2 cup orzo or small pasta
Olive oil

1 (14-ounce) can chicken
   stock or broth
4 slices bacon, chopped
1/4 cup water
2 teaspoons molasses

2 tablespoons balsamic
   vinegar
1 head garlic, roasted
1/3 cup freshly grated
   Parmesan cheese

Sprinkle salt and pepper over the tenderloin. Brown the tenderloin on all sides in 1 tablespoon olive oil in a large sauté pan. Remove the tenderloin to a baking pan, reserving the pan drippings. Bake at 450 degrees for 10 to 15 minutes per pound or until a meat thermometer registers 170 degrees.

Sauté the orzo in a small amount of additional olive oil in a saucepan. Stir in the stock. Cook over medium-low heat for 10 minutes or until the liquid is absorbed.

Render the bacon in the reserved pan drippings and drain. Add the water, molasses and balsamic vinegar to the bacon and mix well. Cook until thickened, stirring constantly.

To serve, squeeze the soft garlic into the orzo. Add the cheese and mix well. Slice the pork as desired. Spoon the orzo in the middle of a serving platter and surround with the sliced pork. Drizzle with the balsamic vinaigrette. Serve with a salad, breadsticks and Merlot or Pinot Noir.

Serves 4 to 6

* *

Baseball got a fast start in Enid when Walter Frantz made it to the major leagues around 1896 and pitched for the St. Louis Cardinals. Following World War I, Enid made a determined bid to become a professional baseball city. In 1920, the Enid Harvesters won the Western Association League Championship.

Big-name players who have performed in Enid include Dizzy Dean, Satchel Paige, and Mickey Mantle. For many years, Enid's Raymond "Rip" Radcliff was among the leading hitters in the American League.

Today, Enid is home to the David Allen Memorial Baseball Park, a glittering new facility that may spark a renewal of interest in the game that thrilled Enid fans for so many years.

Pork with Green Chiles

1 pound pork, cubed
Salt to taste
Flour
1/4 cup (1/2 stick) margarine
3 cups water

1 (14-ounce) can tomato
    wedges
1 (4-ounce) can chopped
    green chiles

1/2 to 1 teaspoon chopped
    canned jalapeño chile
1/4 teaspoon chopped garlic

Sprinkle the pork on all sides with salt and coat with flour. Sauté the pork in the margarine in a deep skillet or large heavy saucepan. Add the water and stir to loosen any browned bits. Simmer for 1 to 2 hours or until the pork is tender, stirring occasionally.

Process the undrained tomatoes in a blender until chunky. Add the tomatoes, green chiles, jalapeño chile and garlic to the pork mixture and mix well. Cook for 1 hour longer, stirring occasionally.

Serves 4

* * * * * * * * * * * * * * * * * * * *

Awesome Spaghetti

2 pounds mild sausage
1 medium onion, chopped
1 green bell pepper,
    chopped
1/4 teaspoon garlic powder
2 (15-ounce) cans tomato
    sauce
2 (12-ounce) cans tomato
    paste

1 (8-ounce) package sliced
    pepperoni
3 cups water
1 (4-ounce) can chopped
    black olives
4 ounces canned or fresh
    sliced mushrooms

2 envelopes spaghetti mix
    with mushrooms
1 teaspoon oregano
1 bay leaf
16 ounces spaghetti, penne
    or pasta of choice,
    cooked, drained

Brown the sausage with the onion, bell pepper and garlic powder in a large saucepan, stirring until the sausage is crumbly; drain. Stir in the tomato sauce, tomato paste, pepperoni, water, olives, mushrooms, spaghetti mix, oregano and bay leaf. Bring to a boil; reduce heat.

Simmer for 1 1/2 to 2 hours or until of the desired consistency, stirring occasionally. Discard the bay leaf. Spoon the sauce over hot cooked spaghetti on a platter.

Serves 8

Ham, Glorious Ham with Burgundy Dijon Glaze

To PREPARE A WHOLE HAM, remove the wrapping and submerge the entire ham in a container filled with water. Chill for 8 to 10 hours. This is the best prescription for dealing with those super-salty hams. Drain the ham and arrange in a large roasting pan. Roast, covered, at 450 degrees for 30 minutes. Turn off the oven. Let the ham stand in the oven with the door closed for 3 hours.

Remove the ham from the oven. Discard the tough outer skin. Trim as much fat as possible. Score the surface of the ham diagonally and stud with cloves. Skim the fat from the pan drippings, reserving the pan drippings. Place the ham in an extra-large oven brown-in-bag. Pour the glaze over the ham. Chill overnight or for at least 4 to 8 hours. Roast using oven bag directions.

To PREPARE A BONELESS HEAT-AND-EAT HAM, place the ham in an oven brown-in-bag and cover the ham with the Burgundy Dijon Glaze several days in advance of roasting. Do not make holes in the bag until just before roasting so that prior to baking you have a great marinating bag with little mess. Marinate in the refrigerator. Roast at 325 degrees for 1 to 1 1/2 hours, depending on the size of the ham. There will be some nice juices in the bag, which can be poured into a heavy saucepan. There is little fat to discard with this variety of ham. Add about 2 cups additional juice, broth or wine to the juices and simmer to reduce the liquid and intensify the flavor. Serve as you would a gravy and spoon over the ham at serving time. This ham may be reheated after church or prepared early in the day and kept warm.

Each Easter, I purchase a good Oklahoma ham, usually a whole Schwab's brand. There are several delicious Oklahoma varieties on the market. On occasion, we are sent one of those salty Tennessee or Virginia varieties, and one must consider just how to make use of them. The Oklahoma hams are MUCH better. Roast at 325 degrees according to brown-in-bag directions. Do not forget to cut holes in the top before baking. Clip a corner of the bag and pour off the juices. Use a separator or chill to make skimming the fat easier. Add the juices to 2 cups red wine. Cook until reduced by half for an intense and sensational "Red Eye Sauce." Leaving the ham in the bag helps keep it warm and allows for an easy transfer.

Burgundy Dijon Glaze

2 cups sugar
1 cup honey

1 cup red wine (burgundy is good)

1/2 cup Dijon mustard

For THE GLAZE, combine the ingredients in a bowl and mix until the consistency of a thick paste.
Variable servings

Contributed by Sherrel Jones

Mediterranean Lamb Chops

Lamb chops, 3/4 to 1 inch thick (1 to 3 per person)

Sherry, red wine or apple juice

Balsamic vinegar

1/4 cup plum or currant jelly

Sprigs of fresh rosemary

Sear the lamb chops in a hot lightly seasoned heavy skillet or grill pan over medium-high heat for 4 to 6 minutes per side. Chopped fresh rosemary leaves and garlic may be added while searing, along with sea salt and freshly ground pepper or lemon pepper, which usually includes some salt. Remove the chops to a heated ovenproof platter and cover. Keep warm in a 275-degree oven. Deglaze the pan with the sherry, adding about 1/3 cup per person. Add a dash of balsamic vinegar. Cook until reduced, stirring constantly. Stir in the jelly. Cook until blended and heated through, stirring constantly. Pour over the chops and top with sprigs of fresh rosemary. Serve with mint jelly or fruit chutney.

Variable servings

Contributed by Sherrel Jones

★ ★

Sherrel Jones has made food a business since serving as the editor of the original "Stir-Ups" and catering for causes from wildflower planting to cooking for the hungry. She has authored a number of food articles and also has done food photography and food styling for various publications and advertisements.

She and her husband Stephen were the focus of a feature article in Southern Living *magazine in May, 1987. Of course Sherrel chose a number of "Stir-Ups" favorites to use in the article. She also developed a marketing video to promote "Stir-Ups." It was the first league to produce a promotional video to accompany the widely acclaimed "Stir-Ups" cookbook.*

She has given cooking demonstrations since the age of nine through 4-H Club activities and teaches from her kitchen at Elmstead Farm through her cooking school, "Just Delicious!" She has studied cooking extensively in the United States and abroad, yet remains a proud promoter and fan of foods grown and produced in Oklahoma. Sherrel's popular column, "A Passion for Food," appears weekly in the food section of The Oklahoman. *She and Stephen have four children.*

Tuscan-Style Grilled Lake Fish with Olive Oil, Lemon and Capers

FISH
Fish fillets
Olive oil
Juice and grated zest of
    lemons (1 for every
    2 fillets)
Capers and sea salt
    to taste

GREMOLATA
Parsley
Garlic
Lemons
Olive oil

FOR THE FISH, this taste of Tuscany is easily done with a grill pan indoors or with a fish basket on the grill outdoors. I use the freshest fish I can find. Good crappie, bass or catfish works well. If using catfish, the farm-raised is much tastier. Talapia would work, as would red snapper. The snapper is ideal for grilling. Because of its firmness, it is less likely to require a basket. I have also grilled good pieces of tuna steaks using this method, as well as swordfish. Begin by washing the fillets to remove any residue. Pat dry with paper towels. (I often cut the fillets diagonally into halves if they are too large. This makes turning and handling easier.) Place the fillets in a sealable plastic bag and add 2 teaspoons of olive oil per fillet and seal tightly. Toss to coat.

Preheat the grill pan. Brush the surface of the pan lightly with olive oil. Arrange the fillets skin side down in the pan. Make sure the pan sizzles slightly when the fillets are placed in the pan. This is an indication that the pan is the right temperature. The fillets are less likely to stick with the flat or skin side next to the pan.

The flesh of the fillets will begin to whiten after 3 or 4 minutes. Turn the fish carefully. Cook for another 3 or 4 minutes. Cooking several fillets at a time will take slightly longer. I find a good strong medium flame works well. Remember every stove is different. Remove from heat. Drizzle the fillets with lemon juice and sprinkle with lemon zest, undrained capers and sea salt. Sprinkle with lemon pepper if you are really crazy about lemon. (This strays from the tradition of Tuscany.)

FOR THE GREMOLATA, rinse parsley to remove all grit. Separate the woody stems and leaves. You will need about 1 cup of loosely packed parsley leaves for each lemon. Pulse in a food processor until coarsely chopped. Mince or crush a couple of garlic cloves and add to the parsley. Peel the outer skin from the lemons with a vegetable peeler, being careful not to remove the white pith as it is quite bitter. Add to the parsley mixture. Add olive oil 1 tablespoon at a time. Pulse just until mixed and of the consistency of a textured paste. Spoon a small amount of the gremolata next to each fillet, or serve traditionally with Osso Bucco or soups.

Variable servings

Contributed by Sherrel Jones

Shirley Bellmon's Homemade Chicken and Noodles

1 (3-pound) chicken
3 bay leaves
2 ribs celery, cut into 3-inch
  pieces

3 egg yolks
1 egg
3 tablespoons ice water

1 teaspoon salt
1 cup flour
Salt and pepper to taste

Combine the chicken, bay leaves and celery with enough water to cover in a stockpot. Bring to a boil; reduce the heat to medium. Cook until the chicken is tender. Remove from heat.

Whisk the egg yolks and egg in a bowl until pale yellow. Add the ice water and salt and whisk until mixed. Add the flour gradually, mixing constantly with a wooden spoon until a stiff dough forms. Divide the dough into 3 equal portions.

Roll each portion 1/8 inch thick on a lightly floured surface. Let stand for a few minutes to dry. Roll each portion as for a jelly roll and cut into 1/2-inch-wide slices with a sharp knife. Shake out each noodle and mix with the remaining flour used for rolling out the noodles. The extra flour on the noodles will thicken the broth.

Remove the chicken and bay leaves from the broth, discarding the bay leaves. Skim the foam from the broth. Chop the chicken into bite-size pieces, discarding the skin and bones. Bring the broth to a boil and add the chopped chicken. Add the noodles in batches, allowing the broth to remain hot. Season with salt and pepper. Simmer for 1 hour or longer. Serve with mashed potatoes for a true comfort food experience.

Serves 4 to 6

Quick Clean-Up Chicken

4 chicken breasts
Seasoned salt and pepper
  to taste

1 yellow squash or zucchini,
  sliced
4 carrots, sliced

2 potatoes, cut into chunks
4 tablespoons butter
8 tablespoons chicken broth

Cut 4 squares of foil large enough to enclose the chicken and vegetables. Place 1 chicken breast on each square. Sprinkle with seasoned salt and pepper. Layer each chicken breast with 1/4 of the vegetables, 1 tablespoon of the butter and 2 tablespoons of the broth. Seal tightly to form a packet.

Arrange the packets on a baking sheet. Bake at 350 degrees for 40 to 45 minutes or until the chicken is cooked through. Open the packets carefully to avoid the steam and drain the juices.

Serves 4

* *

Chicken Kabobs

1/2 cup soy sauce
1/2 cup pineapple juice
1/4 cup vegetable oil
1 teaspoon dry mustard
1 teaspoon brown sugar
1 teaspoon ginger

1 teaspoon garlic powder
3 pounds boneless skinless
  chicken breasts, cubed
1 red onion, cut into chunks
2 green bell peppers,
  cut into chunks

1 (20-ounce) can pineapple
  chunks, drained
1 (6-ounce) can whole
  mushrooms, drained

Combine the soy sauce, pineapple juice, oil, dry mustard, brown sugar, ginger and garlic powder in a shallow dish and mix well. Add the chicken, turning to coat. Marinate, covered, in the refrigerator for 1 to 4 hours, turning occasionally. Drain, discarding the marinade.

Skewer the chicken, onion, bell peppers, pineapple chunks and mushrooms alternately on bamboo skewers. Spray the cold grill rack with nonstick cooking spray to prevent the kabobs from sticking to the rack. Grill the kabobs over hot coals until the chicken is cooked through, turning occasionally.

Serves 8 to 10

Aegean Chicken

4 boneless skinless chicken
    breasts
1/4 cup flour
1/2 teaspoon salt
1/4 teaspoon pepper
1 (6-ounce) jar marinated
    artichoke hearts

2 to 4 tablespoons olive oil
2 tablespoons butter
8 ounces mushrooms, cut
    into quarters
1 (16-ounce) can diced
    tomatoes
2 garlic cloves, minced

1 teaspoon salt
1/2 teaspoon oregano
1/4 teaspoon basil
1/4 teaspoon pepper
3 tablespoons dry sherry
1 cup drained black olives

Cut each chicken breast into 2 or 3 pieces. Pound the chicken about 1/4 inch thick between sheets of waxed paper with a meat mallet. Coat the chicken with a mixture of the flour, 1/2 teaspoon salt and 1/4 teaspoon pepper.

Drain the artichokes, reserving the marinade. Heat the reserved marinade and olive oil in a sauté pan over medium heat. Brown the chicken lightly in the olive oil mixture in the pan. Spoon the chicken into a 9×13-inch baking dish, reserving the pan drippings. Add the butter to the reserved drippings. Heat until the butter melts. Stir in the mushrooms.

Sauté for 3 minutes. Remove the mushrooms to a bowl. Add the undrained tomatoes, garlic, 1 teaspoon salt, oregano, basil and 1/4 teaspoon pepper to the sauté pan. Simmer for 10 minutes, stirring occasionally. Pour the tomato mixture over the chicken. Drizzle with the sherry. Bake at 350 degrees for 15 minutes.

Add the artichokes and olives to the mushrooms and mix gently. Add the artichoke mixture to the chicken mixture and mix well. Bake for 10 minutes longer or until bubbly. Spoon over hot cooked brown or white rice. May be prepared in advance and stored, covered, in the refrigerator. Bring to room temperature and bake as directed.

Serves 4 to 6

Chicken Ro-Tel

6 whole chicken breasts
2 quarts water
12 ounces vermicelli
2 green bell peppers, chopped
2 large onions, chopped

3/4 cup (1 1/2 sticks) margarine
2 (10-ounce) cans Ro-Tel tomatoes
2 pounds Velveeta cheese, cubed

1 (20-ounce) can peas, or frozen peas
1 (6-ounce) can sliced mushrooms, drained
1/2 cup chopped black olives
1/4 cup sliced stuffed olives

Combine the chicken with the water in a stockpot. Bring to a boil. Boil until the chicken is tender. Remove the chicken to a plate with a slotted spoon, reserving 1 1/2 quarts of the broth. Chop the chicken into bite-size pieces, discarding the skin and bones. Bring the reserved broth to a boil. Add the pasta. Cook using package directions until tender; do not drain. Sauté the bell peppers and onions in the margarine in a skillet. Add the chicken, undrained bell pepper mixture and undrained tomatoes to the pasta and mix well. Stir in the cheese, peas, mushrooms and olives.

Spoon the pasta mixture into two 9×13-inch baking dishes. Bake at 350 degrees for 45 minutes or until brown and bubbly. Freeze if desired before baking for future use.

Serves 20

* *

Making Flavored Butters

Use these creamy mixtures to dress up vegetables, meats, and breads. Or melt them to pour over popped popcorn.

*For **Basic Butter Base**, cut up 1/2 cup butter or margarine, place in an ovenproof bowl, and set into a cool oven. Turn the oven to 350 degrees. Heat about 3 minutes in an electric oven (4 minutes in a gas oven) or just until softened. Or, micro-cook on 10% power (low) for 1 to 1 1/2 minutes. Transfer butter to a cool bowl.*

*For **Cajun Butter**, add 1/4 teaspoon ground red pepper, 1/8 teaspoon black pepper, 1/8 teaspoon garlic powder and 1/8 teaspoon dried thyme, crushed, to the butter base and mix well.*

Chicken Enchiladas

1/2 cup chopped onion

1/4 cup (1/2 stick) butter or margarine

1 (8-ounce) can diced green chiles, drained

6 ounces cream cheese, softened

2 tablespoons milk

1/2 teaspoon cumin

4 cups chopped cooked chicken

12 (7-inch) flour tortillas

1 (10-ounce) can cream of chicken soup

1 cup sour cream

1 cup milk

3/4 cup shredded Monterey Jack cheese or Cheddar cheese

Sauté the onion in the butter in a skillet over medium heat until browned. Remove from heat. Stir in 1 tablespoon of the green chiles. Combine the cream cheese, 2 tablespoons milk and cumin in a bowl and mix well. Stir in the chicken and onion mixture.

Spoon about 3 tablespoons of the chicken mixture near the edge of each tortilla and roll to enclose the filling. Place the tortillas seam side down in a greased 3-quart baking dish.

Combine the remaining green chiles, soup, sour cream and 1 cup milk in a bowl and mix well. Spoon the soup mixture evenly over the tortillas. Bake, covered with foil, at 350 degrees for 35 minutes or until heated through. Remove the foil and sprinkle with the cheese. Bake just until the cheese melts.

Makes 12 enchiladas

Tarragon Chicken

4 boneless skinless chicken breasts
1/3 cup bread crumbs
1/4 cup grated Parmesan cheese
2 tablespoons parsley
1 teaspoon salt
1/4 teaspoon pepper
1/4 teaspoon paprika

1/4 teaspoon garlic powder
1/8 teaspoon thyme
1 egg, lightly beaten
1 tablespoon water
4 tablespoons (1/2 stick) butter
8 ounces fresh mushrooms, sliced

2 tablespoons flour
1 cup chicken broth
1 teaspoon tarragon
1/2 cup half-and-half
1/2 teaspoon salt
1/4 teaspoon freshly ground pepper

Flatten the chicken between sheets of waxed paper with a meat mallet. Cut each chicken breast into 2 pieces if too large. Combine the bread crumbs, cheese, parsley, 1 teaspoon salt, 1/4 teaspoon pepper, paprika, garlic powder and thyme in a shallow dish and mix well. Whisk the egg and water in a bowl.

Heat 2 tablespoons of the butter in a large sauté pan over medium heat. Dip the chicken in the egg mixture and coat with the bread crumb mixture. Brown the chicken in the butter. Remove the chicken to a platter with a slotted spoon and cover to keep warm.

Add the remaining 2 tablespoons butter to the sauté pan. Stir in the mushrooms. Sauté until tender. Sprinkle the flour over the mushrooms and stir until mixed. Add the broth gradually, stirring constantly. Stir in the tarragon.

Cook until thickened, stirring constantly. Add the half-and-half gradually, stirring constantly. Stir in 1/2 teaspoon salt and 1/4 teaspoon pepper. Return the chicken to the sauté pan. Cook until slightly thickened, stirring frequently. Spoon over hot cooked spinach fettuccini or your favorite pasta.

Serves 4

Chicken and Mushroom Quesadillas

1/4 cup (1/2 stick) butter
2 1/2 teaspoons chili powder
2 garlic cloves, minced
1 teaspoon oregano
4 ounces fresh shiitake
  mushrooms, stems
  removed, sliced

4 ounces button mushrooms,
  sliced
1 1/2 cups shredded cooked
  chicken
2/3 cup finely chopped onion
1/3 cup chopped fresh
  cilantro

2 1/2 cups shredded
  Monterey Jack cheese
Salt and pepper to taste
16 (5-inch) corn tortillas
Olive oil

Heat the butter in a large skillet over medium-high heat. Stir in the chili powder, garlic and oregano. Sauté for 1 minute or until fragrant. Stir in the mushrooms. Sauté for 10 minutes or until the mushrooms are tender. Remove from heat. Add the chicken, onion and cilantro and mix well.

Cool for 10 minutes. Stir in the cheese, salt and pepper. May be prepared to this point up to 8 hours in advance and stored, covered, in the refrigerator.

Brush 1 side of 8 tortillas with olive oil. Arrange the tortillas oil side down on a baking sheet. Spread the chicken mixture evenly over the tortillas. Top with the remaining 8 tortillas and brush the tops with olive oil.

Arrange the quesadillas on the grill rack. Grill over medium heat for 3 minutes per side or until heated through and golden brown, turning once. Cut into wedges and serve with your favorite toppings.

Makes 8 quesadillas

* *

Hot Chicken Salad Casserole

2 cups chopped cooked
  chicken breasts
2 cups chopped celery
1/2 cup slivered almonds

1/2 cup shredded Cheddar
  cheese
2 tablespoons lemon juice
1 tablespoon chopped onion

1/2 teaspoon salt
1/2 teaspoon pepper
1 cup mayonnaise
1 cup crushed potato chips

Combine the chicken, celery, almonds, cheese, lemon juice, onion, salt and pepper in a bowl and mix well. Stir in the mayonnaise. Spoon the chicken mixture into a baking dish. Sprinkle with the potato chips. Bake at 350 degrees until bubbly.

Serves 4

Chicken Tetrazzini

8 ounces vermicelli

8 ounces fresh mushrooms, sliced

6 tablespoons butter

2 tablespoons flour

2 cups chicken broth

1 cup heavy cream

3 tablespoons dry sherry

1/2 teaspoon salt

1/4 teaspoon pepper

1/4 teaspoon nutmeg

1/2 cup sliced black olives

5 cups chopped cooked chicken

1/2 cup grated Parmesan cheese

Shredded mozzarella cheese to taste

Cook the pasta using package directions; drain. Place the pasta in a lightly greased 9×13-inch baking dish. Sauté the mushrooms in 1 tablespoon of the butter in a saucepan. Remove the mushrooms to a bowl.

Heat the remaining 5 tablespoons butter in the same saucepan until melted. Stir in the flour. Cook until smooth and bubbly, stirring constantly. Add the broth gradually, whisking constantly.

Cook over medium heat until thickened, stirring constantly. Add the cream, sherry, salt, pepper and nutmeg, stirring until blended. Remove from heat. Stir in the mushrooms, olives and chicken. Spoon the chicken mixture over the pasta. Sprinkle with the Parmesan cheese and mozzarella cheese. Bake at 350 degrees for 20 to 25 minutes or until bubbly.

Serves 6 to 8

* *

Mexican Chicken and Rice Casserole

2 cups sliced fresh mushrooms

2 tablespoons olive oil

1 (4-ounce) can diced green chiles, drained

1 (16-ounce) jar chunky salsa

2 cups chopped cooked chicken

2 cups cooked rice

1 cup sour cream

2 cups shredded Cheddar or Monterey Jack cheese

Paprika

Sauté the mushrooms in the olive oil in a large skillet. Stir in the green chiles and salsa. Simmer for 5 minutes, stirring occasionally. Reserve 3/4 cup of the mushroom mixture. Spread the remaining mushroom mixture in a 2-quart baking dish. Layer with the chicken.

Combine the reserved mushroom mixture, rice and sour cream in a bowl and mix well. Spread over the prepared layers. Bake at 350 degrees for 25 to 30 minutes or until bubbly. Sprinkle with the cheese and paprika. Bake for 5 minutes longer or until the cheese melts.

Serves 4

Southwest Sandwiches

1/2 cup mayonnaise

1/2 cup sour cream

1/2 cup sliced green onions

1/2 cup chopped black
    olives

1/2 teaspoon chili powder

1/2 teaspoon cumin

1/4 teaspoon salt

1 loaf sourdough French
    bread

Sliced turkey breast

Sliced tomatoes

Sliced avocados

Shredded Monterey Jack
    cheese

Shredded Cheddar cheese

Combine the mayonnaise, sour cream, green onions, olives, chili powder, cumin and salt in a bowl and mix well. Cut the loaf into 8 to 10 slices.

Spread the mayonnaise mixture on 1 side of each slice. Arrange the slices on a baking sheet. Layer each slice with turkey, sliced tomatoes, sliced avocados and shredded cheese. Bake at 350 degrees for 15 minutes.

Makes 8 to 10 open-face sandwiches

✳ ✳

More Flavored Butters

Prepare Basic Butter Base as directed on page 94 and add the following ingredients for different flavored butters.

*For **Garlic Butter**, add 2 garlic cloves, minced, or 1/2 teaspoon garlic powder.*

*For **Parsley Butter**, add 1 tablespoon snipped parsley; 1 teaspoon lemon juice; 1/4 teaspoon dried savory, crushed; and 1/8 teaspoon salt.*

*For **Herb Butter**, add 1/2 teaspoon ground sage and 1/2 teaspoon dried thyme, crushed.*

*For **Lemon Tarragon Butter**, add 1 teaspoon dried tarragon, crushed, and 1/2 teaspoon finely shredded lemon peel.*

*For **Parmesan Butter**, add 2 tablespoons grated Parmesan cheese and 1/2 teaspoon dried basil, crushed.*

*For **Curry Butter**, add 1/2 teaspoon curry powder.*

Olive-Crusted Salmon with Lemon Vinaigrette

SALMON

2 1/2 ounces fresh white bread crumbs

12 pitted black olives, chopped

1 tablespoon olive oil

2 teaspoons tarragon

1 garlic clove, crushed

1 tablespoon butter, melted

4 salad onions, chopped

Salt and pepper to taste

4 (5-ounce) boneless skinless thick fresh salmon fillets

FOR THE SALMON, combine the bread crumbs, olives, olive oil, tarragon, garlic, butter, onions, salt and pepper in a bowl and mix well. Divide the bread crumb mixture into 4 equal portions. Pat 1 portion over the surface of each fillet.

Arrange the fillets in a single layer on a lightly greased baking sheet. Bake at 375 degrees for 25 minutes or until the salmon flakes easily.

FOR THE VINAIGRETTE, combine the lemon juice, olive oil, mustard and sugar in a jar with a tight-fitting lid and seal tightly. Shake to mix. Drizzle over the salmon just before serving.

Serves 4

LEMON VINAIGRETTE

Juice of 1/2 lemon

1 tablespoon olive oil

1/4 teaspoon whole grain mustard

1/8 teaspoon sugar

* *

Herb Vinegar

Herb vinegar gives salads a gourmet touch. To make herb vinegar, place 2 cups packed fresh tarragon, thyme, dill, mint, or basil in a hot, clean 1-quart jar. Heat 2 cups wine vinegar in a stainless steel or enamel saucepan until hot but not boiling. Pour hot vinegar into the jar over the herb. Cover loosely with a lid or plastic wrap until mixture cools, then cover tightly with the lid. (If using metal lid, cover jar with plastic wrap, then lid.) Let stand in a cool, dark place for 1 week. Remove herb from jar. Transfer vinegar to a clean 1-pint jar. Add a sprig of fresh herb if desired. Cover as above. Store in a cool, dark place for up to 3 months.
Makes 2 cups (thirty-two 1-tablespoon servings)

Scalloped Oysters

1 1/2 pints canned oysters
4 1/2 cups saltine cracker crumbs

1 1/2 cups (3 sticks) butter, melted
3 cups finely chopped celery

1/4 teaspoon salt
1/8 teaspoon pepper
6 tablespoons cream

Drain the oysters, reserving 3/4 cup of the liquor. Toss the cracker crumbs with the butter in a bowl until coated. Cover the bottom of a buttered 9×13-inch baking dish with a thin layer of the crumbs.

Layer the oysters, celery, salt, pepper, reserved oyster liquor and cream 1/2 at a time in the prepared baking dish. Sprinkle with the remaining cracker crumbs. Bake at 400 degrees for 30 minutes or until brown and bubbly.

Serves 8

* *

Seafood with White Wine Sauce

1/4 cup (1/2 stick) butter
8 ounces sea or bay scallops
8 ounces halibut or other firm white fish, cut into 1/2- to 3/4-inch chunks

8 ounces shrimp, peeled, deveined
Salt and pepper to taste
1/4 cup minced shallots
8 mushrooms, thinly sliced

2 small garlic cloves, minced
1/2 cup dry white wine
1 cup cream
2 tablespoons finely chopped parsley

Heat the butter in a large nonstick skillet over medium-high heat until melted. Add the scallops, halibut, shrimp, salt and pepper and mix well. Cook just until the seafood is opaque, stirring frequently with a wooden spoon. Stir in the shallots, mushrooms and garlic.

Cook for 1 minute, stirring frequently. Transfer the seafood mixture to a heated serving dish with a slotted spoon, reserving the pan juices. Add the wine to the reserved pan juices. Cook over high heat for 1 minute, stirring constantly. Stir in the cream. Cook for 2 minutes longer, stirring constantly. Return the seafood mixture to the skillet and mix well. Remove from heat. Spoon over hot cooked rice or angel hair pasta on a serving platter. Sprinkle with the parsley.

Serves 4 to 6

Spicy Grilled Shrimp

48 large shrimp (2 pounds), peeled, deveined

1/4 cup olive oil

1/4 cup red wine

1/4 cup soy sauce

1/4 cup lemon juice

1/4 cup minced fresh parsley

2 tablespoons Worcestershire sauce

2 tablespoons red wine vinegar

1 tablespoon dry mustard

1 1/2 teaspoons paprika

1 teaspoon grated lemon zest

1 1/2 teaspoons minced garlic, crushed

1/8 teaspoon cayenne pepper

16 (10- to 12-inch) bamboo skewers, soaked in water

Rinse the shrimp and pat dry. Combine the olive oil, wine, soy sauce, lemon juice, parsley, Worcestershire sauce, wine vinegar, dry mustard, paprika, lemon zest, garlic and cayenne pepper in a 9×13-inch dish and mix well. Add the shrimp and toss to coat. Marinate at room temperature for 30 minutes, stirring once. Drain, reserving the marinade.

Thread 6 of the shrimp onto one set of 2 skewers, placing 1 skewer through the meaty part of each shrimp and the other one just above the tail. This will resemble railroad tracks with the shrimp between the rails. Repeat the process with the remaining shrimp.

Bring the reserved marinade to a boil in a saucepan; reduce heat. Simmer for 5 minutes. Grill or broil the shrimp 4 to 6 inches from the heat source for 1 1/2 to 2 minutes per side or until the shrimp turn pink and are barely opaque in the center. Serve over rice pilaf with the reserved marinade.

Serves 8

* *

Enid developed into a great center of oil and gas after the development of the Garber-Covington gas field on September 2, 1905. When eight different companies made the city a distributing point, the need to establish refineries became apparent.

By this time, H. H. Champlin had become interested in the oil business. He leased a farm north of Covington and brought in well after well. He established the Champlin Petroleum Company, which eventually became the largest independent oil producer-distributor in America.

Steak Marinade

3/4 cup vegetable oil
1/4 cup soy sauce
3 tablespoons red wine
  vinegar

3 tablespoons honey
1 1/2 teaspoons garlic
  powder, or 1 garlic
  clove, minced

1 1/2 teaspoons ginger
1 green onion, finely
  chopped

Combine the oil, soy sauce, wine vinegar, honey, garlic powder, ginger and green onion in a bowl and mix well. Pour the marinade over your favorite steak. Marinate, covered, in the refrigerator for 4 to 10 hours, turning occasionally. Will marinate about 3 pounds of steak.

  Makes 1 1/3 to 1 1/2 cups

* *

Whiskey Peppercorn Sauce

3 tablespoons butter
3 tablespoons flour
2 cups beef stock

2 tablespoons whiskey
3 tablespoons green
  peppercorns, or to taste

1/2 teaspoon salt
1/8 teaspoon black pepper

Heat the butter in a small saucepan over low heat until melted. Add the flour, stirring until smooth. Cook until light brown, stirring constantly; do not overcook. Whisk in the stock, whiskey, peppercorns, salt and black pepper.

  Cook until of the desired consistency, stirring constantly. Drizzle over grilled steaks. You may substitute canned beef broth for the beef stock.

  Makes 1 to 1 1/2 cups

Oklahoma Barbecue Sauce

2 medium onions, chopped
2 garlic cloves, minced
1/2 cup (1 stick) butter
1 (8- to 10-ounce) bottle
    ketchup
1 (8-ounce) can tomato
    sauce

1/2 cup water
6 tablespoons brown sugar
6 tablespoons
    Worcestershire sauce
1/4 cup vinegar
1 tablespoon prepared
    mustard

2 tablespoons lemon juice
1 teaspoon black pepper
1 teaspoon salt
1 teaspoon red pepper, or
    to taste
1/4 teaspoon Tabasco sauce,
    or to taste

Sauté the onions and garlic in the butter in a large saucepan until the onions are brown. Stir in the ketchup and tomato sauce.

Rinse the ketchup bottle and the tomato sauce can with the water and add to the onion mixture. Stir in the brown sugar, Worcestershire sauce, vinegar, prepared mustard, lemon juice, black pepper, salt, red pepper and Tabasco sauce. Simmer covered, for 30 minutes, stirring occasionally. You may substitute lime juice for the lemon juice.

Makes 1 quart

* *

Shrimp or Chicken Marinade

1/2 cup vegetable oil
1/2 cup soy sauce
1/4 cup white wine
1/2 teaspoon pepper

2 tablespoons finely
    chopped onion
1 to 2 tablespoons finely
    chopped cilantro

1 or 2 garlic cloves, finely
    chopped, or to taste
1/4 teaspoon lemon juice

Combine the oil, soy sauce, wine, pepper, onion, cilantro, garllic and lemon juice in a bowl and mix well. Use as a marinade over shrimp or chicken. Use a food chopper or food processor to finely chop the garlic and onion so it will adhere to the shrimp or poultry during the grilling process.

Makes 1 1/4 cups

Cooking Meat and Poultry

Roasting
* Use tender cuts of beef, veal, pork, or lamb, and young birds.
* Place meat fat side up, or poultry breast side up, on rack in foil-lined shallow roasting pan. Do not add water; do not cover.
* Insert meat thermometer in center of thickest part of meat, being careful that end does not touch bone, fat, or gristle.
* Roast at 300 to 350 degrees until done to taste.

Broiling
* Use tender beef steaks, lamb chops, sliced ham, ground meats, and poultry quarters or halves. Fresh pork should be broiled slowly to insure complete cooking in center. Steaks and chops should be at least 1/2 inch thick.
* Preheat oven to broil. Place meat on rack in foil-lined broiler pan.
* Place pan on oven rack 2 to 5 inches from the heat source, with thicker meat placed the greater distance. Brush poultry with butter.
* Broil until top side is browned; season with salt and pepper.
* Turn; brown second side. Season and serve at once.

Pan Broiling
* Use the same meat and poultry cuts suitable for broiling.
* Place skillet or griddle over medium-high heat. Preheat until a drop of water dances on the surface.
* Place meat in skillet; reduce heat to medium. Do not add water or cover. The cold meat will stick at first, but as it browns it will loosen. If juices start to cook out of the meat, increase heat slightly.
* When meat is brown on one side, turn and brown second side.

Pan Frying
* Use comparatively thin pieces of meat, meat that has been tenderized by pounding or scoring, meat that is breaded, and poultry parts.
* Place skillet over medium-high heat. Add a small amount of shortening—2 tablespoons will usually be sufficient.
* Add meat or poultry when shortening is hot. Cook as in pan broiling.

Braising
* Use for less tender cuts of meat or older birds. You can also braise pork chops, steaks, and cutlets; veal chops, steaks, and cutlets; and poultry legs and thighs.
* Brown meat on all sides as in pan frying. Season with salt and pepper.
* Add a small amount of water—or none if sufficient juices have already cooked out of the meat. Cover tightly.
* Reduce heat to low. Cook until tender, turning occasionally. Meats will cook in their own juices.

Cooking in Liquid
* Use less tender cuts of meat and stewing chickens. Browning of large cuts or whole birds is optional, but it does develop flavor and improve the color.
* Add water or stock to cover meat. Simmer, covered, until tender.
* Add vegetables to allow time to cook without becoming mushy.

Vegetables & Side Dishes

Asparagus Casserole

2 (15-ounce) cans asparagus
spears
2 tablespoons butter
2 tablespoons flour
3/4 cup light cream

3 ounces cream cheese with
chives, diced
1/2 cup blanched almonds,
chopped
Salt and pepper to taste

1/4 cup chopped fresh
parsley
1/2 cup bread crumbs
2 tablespoons butter

Drain the asparagus, reserving 3/4 cup of the liquid. Arrange the asparagus in a 9×13-inch baking dish. Heat 2 tablespoons butter in a saucepan until melted. Stir in the flour. Cook until smooth and bubbly, stirring constantly. Add the cream and reserved asparagus liquid gradually, stirring constantly.

Cook over low heat until the sauce begins to thicken, stirring constantly. Stir in the cream cheese, almonds, salt, pepper and parsley. Cook until the cream cheese melts, stirring constantly. Pour the sauce over the asparagus. Sprinkle with the bread crumbs and dot with 2 tablespoons butter.

Bake at 400 degrees for 15 minutes or until heated through. You may prepare one day in advance and store, covered, in the refrigerator. Bake just before serving, allowing extra baking time.

Serves 4 to 6

* * * * * * * * * * * * * * * * * * * *

Fresh Green Beans in a Pouch

2 pounds fresh green
beans or asparagus,
trimmed

8 ounces fresh mushrooms,
sliced (optional)
1/2 cup (1 stick) butter, sliced

1/2 cup soy sauce
3 garlic cloves, crushed
Salt and pepper to taste

Place a 2-foot sheet of heavy-duty foil on a baking sheet. Mound the green beans and mushrooms in the center of the foil. Pull up the foil edges to form a shallow bowl. Dot the beans with the butter.

Mix the soy sauce and garlic in a small bowl and pour over the beans. Sprinkle with salt and pepper. Bring the foil edges up and together and fold over to form a pouch; seal tightly. Grill over hot coals for 30 to 40 minutes or bake at 350 degrees for 45 minutes. Serve directly from the foil pouch or spoon the vegetables into a serving bowl.

Serves 4 to 6

Oklahoma Baked Beans

1 (16-ounce) can kidney beans or pinto beans
1 (16-ounce) can pork and beans
1 onion, chopped

6 to 8 slices bacon, crisp-cooked, crumbled
1/2 cup ketchup
1/2 cup packed brown sugar

1/2 teaspoon chili powder
1/4 teaspoon cumin
1 cup shredded sharp Cheddar cheese

Drain the kidney beans slightly. Combine the kidney beans, pork and beans, onion, bacon, ketchup, brown sugar, chili powder and cumin in a bowl and mix well. Spoon the bean mixture into a baking dish.

Bake at 400 degrees for 45 minutes. Sprinkle with the cheese. Bake, covered, for 15 minutes longer. Serves 4 to 6

* *

Five-Bean Bake

SAUCE
1/2 cup ketchup
1/2 cup packed brown sugar
2 tablespoons vinegar
1 tablespoon Worcestershire sauce
1 1/2 teaspoons salt
1 teaspoon dry mustard

FOR THE SAUCE, combine the ketchup, brown sugar, vinegar, Worcestershire sauce, salt and dry mustard in a bowl and mix well.

FOR THE BEANS, combine the beans, sausage and onion in a bowl and mix well. Stir in the sauce. Spoon the bean mixture into a 9×13-inch baking dish. Top with the bacon. Bake at 350 degrees for 45 to 60 minutes.

Serves 10 to 12

BEANS
1 (16-ounce) can baked beans
1 (14-ounce) can green beans, drained
1 (14-ounce) can kidney beans, drained
1 (14-ounce) can yellow or wax beans, drained
1 (14-ounce) can black beans, drained, rinsed
1 thin-skin smoked or Polish sausage, chopped
1 small onion, chopped
5 or 6 slices bacon, chopped if desired

Broccoli Bake

1 large head broccoli, or
   3 (10-ounce) packages
   frozen broccoli

16 ounces Velveeta cheese,
   cubed
1 (10-ounce) can cream of
   mushroom soup

1 teaspoon garlic powder
1 package corn bread
   stuffing mix

Discard the tough end of the broccoli stalk. Separate into florets and slice the tender part of the stalk. Steam the fresh broccoli just until al dente or cook the frozen broccoli in a saucepan for 2 minutes; drain. Arrange the broccoli in a 1¹/2-quart baking dish.

Combine the cheese, soup and garlic powder in a double boiler. Cook until the cheese melts, stirring frequently. Pour over the broccoli. Sprinkle with the stuffing mix. Bake at 350 degrees for 30 minutes or until brown and bubbly. Let stand for 5 minutes before serving.

Serves 4 to 6

* *

Marinated Carrots Olé

2 pounds baby carrots
4 large garlic cloves
1¹/2 teaspoons oregano
1 teaspoon coriander
1 teaspoon salt

³/4 teaspoon cumin seeds
¹/4 teaspoon crushed red
   pepper flakes
¹/4 teaspoon freshly ground
   black pepper

1¹/2 tablespoons wine
   vinegar
¹/2 cup olive oil
2 teaspoons chopped fresh
   parsley

Blanch the carrots in boiling water in a saucepan for 2 minutes. Drain the carrots and immediately immerse in a bowl of ice water to stop the cooking process; drain.

Process the garlic, oregano, coriander, salt, cumin seeds, red pepper and black pepper in a food processor until ground. Add the vinegar. Process until of a paste consistency. Add the olive oil gradually, processing constantly until blended. Add the marinade and parsley to the carrots and toss to mix. Marinate at room temperature for 2 hours or longer. Serve at room temperature.

Serves 8 to 10

Celery Amandine

1 chicken bouillon cube
1/2 cup hot water
4 cups sliced celery
1 cup flour
1 tablespoon grated onion

1 tablespoon chopped fresh
   chives
1 1/4 cups half-and-half or
   light cream

1 cup slivered almonds,
   toasted
Salt and pepper to taste

Dissolve the bouillon cube in the hot water. Combine the celery with enough water to cover in a saucepan. Cook until tender; drain. Spoon the celery into a serving bowl.

Combine the flour, onion and chives in a saucepan and mix well. Stir in the bouillon and half-and-half. Cook over low heat until thickened, stirring constantly. Stir in the almonds. Season with salt and pepper. Pour over the celery and mix gently.

Serves 4 to 6

✶ ✶

Gulliver's Creamed Corn

2 (20-ounce) packages
   frozen whole kernel corn
1 cup whipping cream
1 cup milk

2 tablespoons sugar
1 teaspoon salt
1/8 teaspoon white or
   cayenne pepper

1/4 teaspoon MSG
6 tablespoons margarine,
   melted
2 tablespoons flour

Combine the corn, whipping cream, milk, sugar, salt, white pepper and MSG in a 4-quart saucepan and mix well. Bring to a boil; reduce heat. Cook for 5 minutes, stirring occasionally.

Combine the margarine and flour in a bowl and mix until smooth. Add to the corn mixture, stirring constantly. Cook just until heated through and slightly thickened, stirring frequently.

Serves 12

Dill Potatoes

6 potatoes, cooked, peeled,
    sliced
2 tablespoons butter
2 tablespoons flour

1 cup milk
1 1/2 teaspoons salt
1/2 cup mayonnaise

1 teaspoon dillweed
1 teaspoon chopped onion
1/4 teaspoon pepper

Layer the sliced potatoes in a 9×13-inch baking dish. Heat the butter in a saucepan over medium heat until melted. Add the flour, stirring until smooth. Stir in the milk and salt. Cook until thickened, stirring constantly.

Combine the mayonnaise, dillweed, onion and pepper in a bowl and mix well. Stir the mayonnaise mixture into the sauce. Spoon the dill sauce over the potatoes. Bake at 350 degrees for 30 minutes. For variety use cooked unpeeled red potatoes.

Serves 6 to 8

* *

Make-Ahead Mashed Potatoes

5 pounds potatoes, peeled
8 ounces cream cheese,
    softened
1/2 cup half-and-half

1 teaspoon onion salt
1 teaspoon seasoned salt
1 teaspoon salt

1/4 teaspoon pepper
1/2 cup (1 stick) butter,
    softened

Combine the potatoes with enough water to cover in a stockpot. Bring to a boil. Boil until tender; drain.

Beat the cream cheese, half-and-half, onion salt, seasoned salt, salt and pepper in a mixing bowl until creamy, scraping the bowl occasionally. Add the hot potatoes. Beat just until blended. Beat in the butter. Spoon the potato mixture into a buttered 9×13-inch baking dish. Chill, covered, until just before serving time.

Bake at 350 degrees for 30 minutes. May be prepared and frozen, covered, for future use. Thaw in the refrigerator before baking. Prepare 1 hour in advance and keep warm in a slow cooker on Low if desired.

Serves 10

Stuffed Baked Potatoes

3 large baking potatoes
Vegetable oil
1/2 cup sliced green onions
1/4 cup (1/2 stick) butter
1/2 cup light cream

1/2 cup sour cream
1 teaspoon salt
1/2 teaspoon white pepper
1 cup shredded Cheddar
    cheese

1/4 cup (1/2 stick) butter,
    melted
Paprika

Rub the entire surface of the potatoes with oil and pierce with a fork. Bake at 400 degrees for 1 hour or until tender. Let stand until cool to the touch. Cut the potatoes lengthwise into halves. Scoop the pulp carefully into a mixing bowl, leaving a thin shell.

Sauté the green onions in 1/4 cup butter in a skillet until tender. Add the green onions, light cream, sour cream, salt and white pepper to the potato pulp. Beat until well mixed. Fold in the cheese.

Spoon the potato mixture into the shells. Place the shells in a 9×13-inch baking pan. Drizzle with 1/4 cup melted butter and sprinkle with paprika. Bake at 350 degrees for 20 to 30 minutes or until heated through.

Serves 6

Spinach and Artichoke Casserole

3 (6-ounce) jars marinated
    artichokes, drained
3 (10-ounce) packages
    frozen chopped spinach,
    thawed, drained

9 ounces cream cheese,
    softened
1/4 cup (1/2 stick) butter,
    softened
1/2 cup milk

Juice of 1/2 lemon
Garlic salt to taste
Pepper to taste
1/2 cup grated Parmesan
    cheese

Cut the artichokes into halves if needed and arrange over the bottom of a 9×13-inch baking dish. Press the spinach to remove excess moisture. Layer the spinach over the artichokes.

Blend the cream cheese, butter, milk, lemon juice, garlic salt and pepper in a mixing bowl, adding additional milk if needed for a spreading consistency. Spread the cream cheese mixture over the spinach and sprinkle with the Parmesan cheese. Bake at 375 degrees for 25 minutes. The flavor is enhanced if prepared in advance and stored, covered, in the refrigerator for 6 to 24 hours before baking.

Serves 6 to 8

Oklahoma Spinach Rockefeller

1 (10-ounce) package frozen
    chopped spinach
1/2 cup milk
1/2 cup cubed sharp
    Cheddar cheese

Juice of 1 lemon
6 green onions, chopped
2 tablespoons butter
1 teaspoon Louisiana hot
    sauce

1 teaspoon salt
1 egg, beaten
1/4 cup grated Parmesan
    cheese

Cook the spinach using package directions, omitting the salt; drain. Press the spinach to remove the excess moisture. Combine the spinach, milk, Cheddar cheese, lemon juice, green onions, butter, hot sauce and salt in a saucepan.

Cook until the cheese melts, stirring frequently. Remove from heat. Let stand until cool. Stir in the egg. Spoon the spinach mixture into 4 buttered ramekins or a 1-quart baking dish. Sprinkle with the Parmesan cheese. Bake at 350 degrees for 20 minutes.

Serves 4

* * * * * * * * * * * * * * * * * * * *

Pecan-Topped Sweet Potatoes

4 pounds sweet potatoes,
    peeled, cooked, mashed
3/4 cup sugar
2 eggs, beaten

1/2 cup (1 stick) butter,
    softened
1 tablespoon vanilla extract
1 cup packed brown sugar

1/3 cup flour
1/3 cup butter, softened
1 cup pecans, chopped

Combine the sweet potatoes, sugar, eggs, 1/2 cup butter and vanilla in a bowl and mix until blended. Spoon the mixture into a 9×13-inch baking dish.

Combine the brown sugar, flour and 1/3 cup butter in a bowl and mix with a fork until crumbly. Stir in the pecans. Sprinkle the crumb mixture over the sweet potatoes. Bake at 350 degrees for 30 minutes. Serve warm. Double the topping mixture for an extra-sweet and crunchy treat.

Serves 8 to 10

Baked Vegetable Medley

1 large package frozen
  mixed vegetables
1 cup chopped onion, or
  to taste

1 cup chopped celery
1 cup shredded cheese
1 cup mayonnaise

1 sleeve saltine crackers,
  crushed
1/2 cup (1 stick) butter,
  melted

Cook the mixed vegetables using package directions; drain. Spoon the mixed vegetables into a baking dish.

Combine the onion, celery, cheese and mayonnaise in a bowl and mix well. Spread the mayonnaise mixture over the vegetables. Sprinkle with a mixture of the cracker crumbs and melted butter. Bake at 350 degrees for 30 minutes.

Serves 6 to 8

* *

Fettuccini Alfredo

2 tablespoons unsalted butter
2 cups heavy whipping
  cream

8 ounces mascarpone
  cheese

1 cup grated Parmesan
  cheese (fresh or canned)
16 ounces fettuccini

Bring enough water to a boil in a saucepan for the pasta. Heat the butter in a medium saucepan until melted. Stir in the whipping cream and mascarpone cheese. Cook until the cheese melts, stirring frequently. Add the Parmesan cheese gradually, stirring constantly.

Cook over low to medium heat for 10 minutes, stirring occasionally. The resulting sauce should be reduced by 1/3 and thickened. Remove from heat.

Add the pasta to the boiling water. Cook using package directions; drain. Add the hot pasta to the sauce gradually, stirring constantly. Cook for 2 to 3 minutes longer or just until heated through, stirring constantly. Add crumbled cooked bacon, cooked shrimp, cooked scallops or crab meat for variety.

Serves 3 as a main dish or 6 as a side dish

Contributed by Rick Tozzi

Linguini alla Puttanesca

1/2 cup olive oil
3 garlic cloves, crushed
1 teaspoon red pepper
    flakes
12 ounces canned tomatoes

2 tablespoons capers
4 ounces kalamata olives,
    sliced
1 teaspoon oregano

1 1/2 inches anchovy paste
    (from tube)
Chopped fresh parsley to taste
Salt and pepper to taste
Hot cooked linguini

Combine the olive oil, garlic and red pepper flakes in a saucepan. Cook until the garlic begins to brown, stirring frequently. Stir in the tomatoes, capers, olives and oregano. Bring to a boil; reduce heat.

Simmer for 25 minutes, stirring occasionally. Add the anchovy paste and mix well. Stir in parsley, salt and pepper. Spoon over linguini on a serving platter.

Little saying in Italy; "if a wife wants her husband to stay home she will make this dish because the aroma is more enticing than a lady of the evening."

Serves 4

Contributed by La Luna Blu Restaurant

* *

Penne with Artichokes

16 ounces (6 cups) penne
1/4 cup olive oil
1 cup undrained marinated
    artichoke hearts, cut into
    quarters

1 cup undrained canned
    Italian tomatoes, chopped
1/4 cup sliced black olives
3/4 cup spicy vegetable juice
    cocktail

1 tablespoon chopped fresh
    basil
Salt and pepper to taste
1/2 cup grated Parmesan
    cheese

Cook the pasta using package directions. Heat the olive oil in a skillet over medium-low heat until a drop of water sizzles when it hits the oil.

Sauté the artichokes, tomatoes and olives in the hot olive oil for 3 to 5 minutes. Stir in the vegetable juice cocktail and basil. Simmer while the pasta is cooking, stirring occasionally. Drain the pasta, add the sauce and toss to coat. Sprinkle with the cheese. Serve immediately. Makes great leftovers and is even good served cold.

Serves 4 to 6

Alfredo Sauce

2 cups whipping cream
4 ounces Parmesan cheese,
    grated, or to taste

1/4 cup (1/2 stick) butter,
    gently melted

2 egg yolks, beaten
Garlic salt to taste
Pepper to taste

Combine the whipping cream, cheese, butter, egg yolks, garlic salt and pepper in a saucepan and mix well. Bring to a gentle boil, whisking constantly. Boil until the sauce is of the desired consistency, whisking constantly. Spoon the sauce over 16 ounces hot cooked pasta on a serving platter.

For variety, add sautéed mushrooms, chopped spinach, chopped cooked bacon, cooked shrimp and/or cooked chicken. Be creative and add your favorite ingredients.

Serves 6 to 8

* * * * * * * * * * * * * * * * * *

Cajun Cream Sauce

1/4 cup water
2 tablespoons cornstarch
2 tablespoons finely
    chopped green onions

3 tablespoons dry white
    wine
1 tablespoon Cajun spice

1 tablespoon gumbo filé
    powder
1/2 teaspoon salt
2 cups heavy cream

Combine the water and cornstarch in a small bowl and mix well. Cook the green onions in the wine in a saucepan over medium heat until tender, stirring frequently. Stir in the Cajun spice, gumbo filé and salt. Add the heavy cream and mix well. Stir in the cornstarch mixture.

Cook until the sauce thickens and is of the desired consistency, stirring constantly. Do not scald the cream. Spoon the sauce over hot cooked pasta on a serving platter. Add cooked shrimp, chicken or sliced smoked sausage for a great entrée.

Makes 2 cups

Tomato Cream Sauce

1 small white onion, minced
1 garlic clove, minced
Olive oil

4 cans Roma tomatoes,
    peeled, seeded, chopped
Salt to taste

1 cup red wine
2 teaspoons Italian seasoning
1 cup heavy cream

Sauté the onion and garlic in olive oil in a 4-quart saucepan. Stir in the tomatoes and salt. Add the wine and Italian seasoning and mix well.

Cook until most of the liquid has evaporated, stirring occasionally. Stir in the heavy cream. Cook until thickened and of the desired consistency, stirring frequently. Spoon the sauce over 16 ounces hot cooked mushroom tortellini or your favorite pasta on a serving platter.

Serves 8

* * * * * * * * * * * * * * * * * * * *

Pasta Sauce with Tomatoes and Prosciutto

15 large ripe plum tomatoes,
    or 1 (35-ounce) can
    Italian tomatoes
4 ounces prosciutto, minced
2 tablespoons olive oil

4 medium white onions,
    chopped
4 garlic cloves, minced
2 tablespoons basil
1 1/2 teaspoons salt

1 tablespoon chopped fresh
    parsley
Hot cooked pasta
1 tablespoon butter

Process the tomatoes in a food processor or food mill until of the desired consistency. Sauté the prosciutto in the olive oil in a saucepan over medium heat until crisp. Stir in the onions, garlic, basil and salt.

Simmer for 3 minutes, stirring occasionally. Add the tomatoes and mix well. Simmer for 20 minutes or until most of the liquid has evaporated and the sauce is of the desired consistency, stirring occasionally. Stir in the parsley. Toss hot cooked pasta with the butter in a bowl. Spoon the sauce over the pasta.

Serves 6 to 8

Chinese Fried Rice

4 slices bacon
2 eggs, beaten
5 tablespoons soy sauce
2 cups shredded cabbage

6 green onions, chopped
3 cups cold cooked rice
2 cups chopped cooked
  meat

1/2 cup chopped water
  chestnuts
Salt and pepper to taste

Fry the bacon in a skillet until crisp. Drain, reserving the bacon drippings. Crumble the bacon. Scramble the eggs in half the reserved bacon drippings in a skillet until the eggs are in pieces the size of peas.

Heat the remaining reserved bacon drippings and soy sauce in a large skillet. Add the cabbage and green onions. Stir-fry just until tender-crisp. Add the rice, stirring until the rice is coated with the soy sauce mixture. Stir in the bacon, eggs, meat and water chestnuts.

Stir-fry until the mixture is heated through. Season with salt and pepper. Reduce the heat to low to keep warm until serving time.

Serves 4

* *

Green Chile Rice

3 (4-ounce) cans green
  chiles, drained
1 cup chopped onion
1/4 cup (1/2 stick) butter or
  margarine

4 cups hot cooked white rice
2 cups sour cream
1 cup small curd creamy
  cottage cheese
1 large bay leaf, crumbled

1/2 teaspoon salt
1/8 teaspoon pepper
2 cups shredded sharp
  Cheddar cheese
Chopped fresh parsley

Slice the chiles lengthwise into halves, leaving the seeds. Sauté the onion in the butter in a large skillet until golden brown. Remove from heat. Stir in the hot rice, sour cream, cottage cheese, bay leaf, salt and pepper.

Layer the rice mixture, chiles and Cheddar cheese 1/2 at a time in a greased 12×18-inch baking dish. Bake at 375 degrees for 25 minutes or until bubbly. Sprinkle with parsley.

Serves 6 to 8

Wild Rice

1 (6-ounce) package
　long grain and
　wild rice
1 broth can water

2 (14-ounce) cans chicken
　broth
4 slices bacon, crisp-cooked,
　crumbled

Bacon drippings to taste
Salt and pepper to taste

Combine the rice, water, broth, bacon, bacon drippings, salt and pepper in a saucepan and mix well. Cook for 30 to 60 minutes or until the rice is tender and the liquid has been absorbed. For variety, add minced onion, chopped celery and/or mushrooms.

Serves 4 to 8

* * * * * * * * * * * * * * * * * * * *

Buttery Walnut Stuffing

12 cups coarse dry bread
　crumbs
1 cup (2 sticks) butter or
　margarine
1 cup sliced celery
1 cup sliced fresh mushrooms

1 cup coarsely chopped
　onion
1 or 2 cups giblet or chicken
　broth
2 teaspoons thyme

1 teaspoon salt
1/2 teaspoon sage
1/4 teaspoon pepper
1 cup coarsely chopped
　walnuts

Spread the bread crumbs in a baking pan. Toast at 350 degrees for 20 minutes or until light brown, stirring once or twice. Heat the butter in a large skillet until melted. Sauté the celery, mushrooms and onion in the butter just until tender. Stir in 1 cup broth, thyme, salt, sage and pepper. (Add 2 cups broth if you plan on baking the stuffing separately.)

Pour the broth mixture over the bread crumbs in a bowl and toss until moistened. Stir in the walnuts. Stuff into the body cavity of a 12-pound turkey. To cook the stuffing separately, spoon the stuffing mixture into a 2-quart baking dish. Bake, covered, at 350 degrees for 30 minutes; remove cover. Bake for 10 to 15 minutes longer or until light brown.

Makes 2 1/2 quarts

Vegetable Saucery

Basic White Sauce

Ingredients	Thin	Medium	Thick
Margarine	2 tablespoons	1/4 cup	6 tablespoons
Flour	2 tablespoons	1/4 cup	6 tablespoons
Milk	2 cups	2 cups	2 cups
Salt	1 teaspoon	1 teaspoon	1 teaspoon

Melt margarine in a saucepan over low heat. Stir in the flour until smooth. Add the milk gradually, stirring constantly. Cook over medium heat until bubbly, stirring constantly. Season with salt. Add pepper to taste.

* Substitute 1 cup chicken broth for 1 cup milk if preferred.
* Substitute evaporated skim milk for whole milk to make Low-Calorie Basic White Sauce.

Variations

Sauce	Add to basic sauce	Use with
Cheese	1/2 cup sharp Cheddar cheese 2 drops of Worcestershire sauce	broccoli, brussels sprouts, cabbage, cauliflower
Curry	2 to 3 teaspoons curry powder 1/8 teaspoon ginger	asparagus, carrots, mushrooms, squash
Dill	1 to 2 teaspoons dillweed	cauliflower, green beans
Mushroom	1/2 cup sautéed mushrooms	broccoli, peas, spinach
Mustard	1 to 2 tablespoons prepared mustard or Dijon mustard	bok choy, green beans, onions, tomatoes
Parsley	2 tablespoons chopped parsley	peas, potatoes
Tomato	1/4 cup chili sauce Dash of Tabasco sauce	eggplant, onions, peppers, zucchini

Brunches & Breads

Brunch Eggs Casserole

1 pound breakfast sausage
(regular or reduced-fat)
2 cups milk
6 eggs
1 1/2 teaspoons dry mustard
1 teaspoon salt

1 teaspoon mild curry
powder (optional)
1/2 teaspoon dillweed
Pepper to taste
2 cups shredded Cheddar
cheese

1 cup fresh or canned sliced
mushrooms
1/2 cup chopped onion
(optional)
6 slices fresh bread, cubed

Brown the sausage in a skillet, stirring until crumbly; drain. Whisk the milk and eggs in a bowl until blended. Whisk in the dry mustard, salt, curry powder, dillweed and pepper. Add the sausage, cheese, mushrooms and onion and mix well. Fold in the bread cubes.

Pour the sausage mixture into a baking dish. Bake at 350 degrees for 40 minutes. You may prepare 1 day in advance and store, covered, in the refrigerator. Bake just before serving.

Serves 8

* *

Dilled Ham and Eggs

1/4 cup minced green onions
3 tablespoons butter
3 tablespoons flour
1/2 teaspoon salt

1/4 teaspoon dillweed
1/8 teaspoon pepper
2 cups milk
2 cups chopped cooked ham

6 hard-cooked eggs, sliced
1 tablespoon chopped fresh
parsley
Toast points

Sauté the green onions in the butter in a skillet. Stir in the flour. Cook over low heat until bubbly, stirring constantly. Add the salt, dillweed and pepper and mix well. Remove from heat.

Add the milk gradually, stirring constantly. Cook until thickened, stirring constantly. Fold in the ham, eggs and parsley. Spoon over toast points on plates.

To prepare toast points, remove the crusts from cracked wheat bread slices. Pat the bread over the bottom and up the side of muffin cups. Toast at 350 degrees until light brown.

Serves 6

Wheat Germ Onion Quiche

WHEAT GERM CRUST

1/4 cup (1/2 stick) butter
2/3 cup flour
1/4 cup wheat germ
4 teaspoons water

FOR THE CRUST, cut the butter into the flour in a bowl until crumbly. Stir in the wheat germ. Sprinkle with the water and stir with a fork until an easily manageable dough forms. Pat the dough over the bottom and up the side of a 9-inch quiche pan. Bake at 425 degrees for 10 minutes.

FOR THE FILLING, sauté the onion in the butter in a skillet for 4 to 5 minutes or until tender. Stir in the wheat germ and wine. Mix the sour cream and egg in a bowl until blended. Stir in the parsley, tarragon and salt. Add the sour cream mixture to the onion mixture and mix well.

Spoon the onion mixture into the baked shell. Sprinkle with the cheese and almonds. Bake at 375 degrees for 25 minutes or until the center is set.

Serves 6

ONION FILLING

1 medium onion, thinly sliced
1/4 cup (1/2 stick) butter
1/2 cup wheat germ
1/4 cup dry white wine
1 cup sour cream
1 egg
1/2 cup minced fresh parsley
1/2 teaspoon tarragon, crushed
1/4 teaspoon salt
1/2 cup shredded Monterey Jack cheese
1/4 cup chopped almonds

* *

Pop-Free Crunchy Bacon

Before frying, take each slice of refrigerated bacon and coat both sides with all-purpose flour. Then fry as usual. The bacon will not curl and shrinks very little. The flour gives it more body and makes a wonderful crunchy crust!

Spinach Quiche

CRUST

1/2 cup (1 stick) butter, softened
4 ounces cream cheese, softened
1 cup flour

FOR THE CRUST, combine the butter, cream cheese and flour in a food processor container. Process until the mixture is of a coarse consistency. Chill, covered, for 15 minutes. Press the dough over the bottom and up the side of a pie plate using waxed paper or plastic wrap. Chill, covered, for 30 minutes.

FOR THE FILLING, press the excess moisture from the spinach. Combine the spinach and flour in a bowl and mix well. Stir in the Swiss cheese, Cheddar cheese, mushrooms, milk, mayonnaise, eggs, green onions and bacon.

Spoon the spinach mixture into the prepared pie plate. Bake at 350 degrees for 60 to 70 minutes or until set.

Serves 6

SPINACH FILLING

1 (10-ounce) package frozen chopped spinach, thawed, drained
2 tablespoons flour
8 ounces Swiss cheese, shredded
8 ounces Cheddar cheese, shredded
8 ounces mushrooms, sliced
1/2 cup milk
1/2 cup mayonnaise
3 eggs, beaten
3 green onions with tops, chopped
4 slices bacon, crisp-cooked, crumbled

Enid is possibly best known as the Wheat Capital. The massive wheat crops from the Great Plains could not all be sold at harvest time and huge storage elevators were the answer for the time. W. B. Johnston, Union Equity, and Pillsbury built enormous grain storage facilities from 1926 to 1954, making Enid the third-largest storage site in America.

Crustless Quiche

1/2 cup chopped onion
2 garlic cloves, chopped
1 tablespoon olive oil
3/4 cup flour
1/4 teaspoon salt

1/4 teaspoon pepper
8 ounces Co-Jack cheese, shredded
1 cup chopped cooked ham

1 (4-ounce) can chopped mushrooms, drained
1 cup milk
2 eggs

Sauté the onion and garlic in the olive oil in a small saucepan until the onion is tender but not brown. Combine the flour, salt and pepper in a bowl and mix well. Stir in the cheese, ham and mushrooms.

Whisk the milk and eggs in a bowl until blended. Stir in the onion mixture. Add the milk mixture to the cheese mixture and mix well. Spoon into a greased 9-inch pie plate. Bake at 425 degrees for 30 minutes. Serve with fresh fruit and muffins.

Serves 6

* *

Honeyed Corn Grits

1 (11-ounce) can white Shoe Peg corn, drained
2 cups water
1 1/2 cups milk

1/2 cup white grits
1/2 cup yellow cornmeal
1 cup half-and-half

1/4 cup (1/2 stick) butter
3/4 teaspoon salt
1/2 cup honey, or to taste

Process the corn in a blender until coarsely chopped. Bring the water and milk to a boil in a 2-quart saucepan. Add the grits and cornmeal, stirring constantly; reduce the heat.

Simmer for 8 to 10 minutes, stirring occasionally. Remove from heat. Stir in the corn, half-and-half, butter and salt. Add the honey and mix well. Serve immediately or spoon the grits mixture into a greased baking dish. Bake at 350 degrees for 30 minutes. The mixture will thicken as it bakes. Top with additional butter before baking for a rich decadent taste.

Serves 4 to 6

Oklahoma Grits

4 cups water
1 cup grits
1 1/2 teaspoons salt
16 ounces Cheddar cheese,
  shredded

1 (4-ounce) can chopped
  green chiles, drained
  (optional)
6 tablespoons butter
3 eggs, beaten

1 tablespoon seasoned salt
1 tablespoon Tabasco sauce,
  or to taste
1/2 teaspoon paprika

Bring the water to a boil in a saucepan. Add the grits and salt gradually, stirring constantly to prevent lumps. Cook until very thick, stirring frequently. Add the cheese, green chiles, butter, eggs, seasoned salt, Tabasco sauce and paprika and mix well.

Spoon the grits into a 2-quart baking dish. Bake at 300 degrees for 45 to 55 minutes. Serve hot.
Serves 4 to 6

★ ★ ★ ★ ★ ★ ★ ★ ★ ★ ★ ★ ★ ★ ★ ★ ★ ★

Fresh Apple Fritters

3 cups flour
2 teaspoons baking powder
1/2 teaspoon salt
1 cup milk
1/4 cup (1/2 stick) butter or
  margarine, melted

1 egg, beaten
Juice and grated zest of
  1 orange
1 cup finely chopped
  unpeeled apple

1/2 cup sugar
1 teaspoon vanilla extract
2 cups vegetable oil
Confectioners' sugar

Sift the flour, baking powder and salt together. Combine the milk, butter and egg in a bowl and mix well. Stir in the orange juice, orange zest, apple, sugar and vanilla. Add the flour mixture and stir just until moistened; do not overmix.

Heat the oil in a skillet to 350 degrees. Drop the batter by tablespoonfuls into the hot oil. Fry until golden brown on both sides; drain. Let stand until cool. Roll in confectioners' sugar. Serve with a salad or as a dessert.
Serves 10 to 12

Blueberry Buckle

TOPPING

1/2 cup sugar

1/3 cup flour

1/2 teaspoon cinnamon

1/4 cup (1/2 stick) butter

*F*OR THE TOPPING, combine the sugar, flour and cinnamon in a bowl and mix well. Cut in the butter until crumbly.

FOR THE BUCKLE, sift the flour, baking powder and salt together. Beat the sugar, shortening and egg in a mixing bowl until creamy. Stir in the milk. Add the flour mixture and beat until smooth. Fold in the blueberries.

Spoon the blueberry mixture into a greased and floured 9×9-inch baking dish. Sprinkle with the topping. Bake at 375 degrees for 45 to 50 minutes or until brown and bubbly.

Serves 9

BUCKLE

2 cups flour

2 teaspoons baking powder

1/2 teaspoon salt

3/4 cup sugar

1/4 cup shortening

1 egg

1/2 cup milk

2 cups fresh or frozen blueberries

* *

Cranberry Shortcake

SHORTCAKE

2 cups flour

1 1/2 cups sugar

2 teaspoons baking powder

1/2 teaspoon salt

1/4 cup (1/2 stick) butter

3 cups frozen cranberries, cut into halves

1 cup milk

*F*OR THE SHORTCAKE, combine the flour, sugar, baking powder and salt in a bowl and mix well. Cut in the butter until crumbly. Stir in the cranberry halves and milk. Spoon the cranberry mixture into a 9×13-inch baking dish. Bake at 350 degrees for 30 minutes.

FOR THE SAUCE, combine the brown sugar, sugar, butter and cream in a saucepan. Bring to a boil, stirring constantly. Pour over the shortcake.

Serves 15

SAUCE

1/2 cup packed brown sugar

1/2 cup sugar

1/2 cup (1 stick) butter

1/2 cup cream

Super Colossal Cinnamon Pecan Ring

1/3 cup sugar

1/3 cup packed brown sugar

2 teaspoons cinnamon

2 (1-pound) loaves frozen
    bread dough, thawed

1/3 cup butter, melted

1/2 cup chopped pecans

1 1/4 cups confectioners'
    sugar

Vanilla extract to taste

4 teaspoons (about) milk

Grease a pizza pan or 12-inch round baking pan. Combine the sugar, brown sugar and cinnamon in a shallow dish or on a large piece of foil. Flatten the bread dough slightly on a lightly floured surface. Cut each loaf into 4 portions. Roll each bread dough portion into an 18-inch rope. Brush 1 rope on all sides with melted butter and coat with some of the sugar mixture. Shape the rope into a coil in the center of the prepared pizza pan. Repeat the buttering and coating process with another rope. Attach the rope securely to the end of the first rope and coil around the first coil. Continue the buttering, coating and coiling process with the remaining ropes to form a 10- to 11-inch circle. Sprinkle any remaining sugar mixture over the top of the dough. Sprinkle with the pecans.

Let rise, covered with plastic wrap, in the refrigerator for 8 to 10 hours or until doubled in size. Let stand at room temperature for 15 to 20 minutes. Bake at 350 degrees for 30 to 35 minutes or until light brown, covering with foil during the last 10 minutes of the baking process to prevent overbrowning. Cool for 15 minutes on a wire rack. Combine the confectioners' sugar, vanilla and enough milk in a bowl to make a thick glaze. Drizzle the glaze over the warm coffee cake. Serve immediately.

Serves 10 to 12

Contributed by Maple Place Bed & Breakfast

Sour Cream Coffee Cake

TOPPING
2 tablespoons brown sugar
1/2 teaspoon cinnamon
Chopped nuts (optional)

COFFEE CAKE
2 cups sifted flour
1 teaspoon baking powder
1/4 teaspoon salt
2 cups sugar
1 cup (2 sticks) butter, softened
1 cup sour cream
2 eggs
1 teaspoon vanilla extract

GLAZE
Confectioners' sugar
Almond extract
Milk

FOR THE TOPPING, combine the brown sugar, cinnamon and nuts in a bowl and mix well. Double the ingredients for a richer coffee cake.

FOR THE COFFEE CAKE, mix the flour, baking powder and salt together. Combine the sugar, butter, sour cream, eggs and vanilla in a mixing bowl. Beat at low speed until creamy, scraping the bowl occasionally. Beat in flour mixture.

Layer the batter and topping 1/2 at a time in a greased and floured bundt pan. Bake at 350 degrees for 35 to 45 minutes or until the side pulls from the edge of the pan. Cool in pan for 10 minutes. Invert onto a cake plate.

FOR THE GLAZE, combine confectioners' sugar and flavoring with enough milk in a bowl to make of a drizzling consistency. Drizzle over the coffee cake.

Serves 15

* * * * * * * * * * * * * * * * * * * *

Orange Crunchy Rolls

Line a baking sheet with foil and brush the foil with margarine. Mix 1 cup sugar and 2 tablespoons grated orange zest in a bowl. Add enough orange juice to moisten. Dip 12 brown and serve rolls in 1/4 cup melted margarine until coated. Arrange the rolls on the prepared baking sheet. Sprinkle with the sugar mixture. Bake using brown and serve package directions.

Pantry Corn Bread

1 (9-ounce) package yellow
   cake mix
1 cup yellow cornmeal
1 cup flour

4 teaspoons baking powder
1/2 teaspoon salt
1 cup milk

1/4 cup (1/2 stick) butter,
   melted
1 egg, beaten

Prepare the cake batter using package directions, being careful to beat air into the mixture. Combine the cornmeal, flour, baking powder and salt in a separate bowl and mix well. Stir in the milk, butter and egg. Fold the cornmeal mixture into the cake batter.

    Spoon the batter into 2 greased 8-inch round baking pans or a 9×13-inch baking pan. Bake at 400 degrees for 20 to 25 minutes or until a wooden pick inserted in the center comes out clean and the top is light brown.

    Serves 12 to 16

* * * * * * * * * * * * * * * * * * *

Baked French Toast

1 loaf firm bread, cubed
8 ounces cream cheese,
   cubed

10 eggs
1 1/2 cups half-and-half

1/2 cup (1 stick) butter,
   melted
1/4 cup maple syrup

Arrange half the bread cubes in a 9×13-inch baking pan sprayed with nonstick cooking spray. Layer with the cream cheese and remaining bread cubes.

    Whisk the eggs, half-and-half, butter and maple syrup in a bowl until blended. Pour the egg mixture over the prepared layers, pressing the bread cubes to ensure even coverage. Chill, covered with plastic wrap, for 8 to 10 hours. Bake at 350 degrees for 40 to 50 minutes or until set. Serve with jam, confectioners' sugar and/or syrup.

    Serves 6

Jamaican Jungle Bread

BREAD

1 1/2 cups flour

1 cup quick-cooking oats

1/2 cup sugar

1 teaspoon baking powder

1 teaspoon baking soda

1 teaspoon cinnamon

1/2 teaspoon salt

1/2 cup flaked coconut

1/2 cup chopped nuts (walnuts, almonds or pecans), toasted

1 cup mashed bananas (about 3 medium)

1 (8-ounce) can crushed pineapple

1/4 cup vegetable oil

2 eggs, beaten

FOR THE BREAD, combine the flour, oats, sugar, baking powder, baking soda, cinnamon and salt in a bowl and mix well. Stir in the coconut and nuts. Combine the bananas, undrained pineapple, oil and eggs in a bowl and mix well. Add the banana mixture to the flour mixture and stir just until moistened. Let stand for 15 minutes.

Spoon the batter into a greased 5x9-inch loaf pan. Bake at 350 degrees for 50 to 55 minutes or until a wooden pick inserted in the center comes out clean. Cool in pan for 5 minutes. Run a knife around the edges of the loaf and invert onto a wire rack to cool.

FOR THE GLAZE, combine the confectioners' sugar, butter, milk and flavoring in a bowl and mix until of a drizzling consistency. Drizzle over the loaf.

Makes 1 loaf

GLAZE (optional)

1/2 cup confectioners' sugar

1 tablespoon butter or margarine, softened

1 to 2 teaspoons milk

1/2 teaspoon coconut or vanilla extract

Biscuit Basics

★ *Mix the dough only a short time—just enough to moisten ingredients.*

★ *Handle dough as little as possible to keep the fat from melting.*

★ *Roll dough thin and fold over once. Biscuits will be crisp on the outside, and flaky in the middle.*

★ *To reheat, place in a well-dampened paper bag in an oven on low (300 degrees).*

Poppy Seed Bread

BREAD

3 cups flour

1 1/2 teaspoons salt

1 1/2 teaspoons baking
  powder

2 1/2 cups sugar

1 1/2 cups milk

1 cup plus 2 tablespoons
  vegetable oil

3 eggs

1 1/2 tablespoons poppy
  seeds

1 1/2 teaspoons each vanilla
  extract, almond extract
  and butter flavoring

FOR THE BREAD, mix the flour, salt and baking powder together. Combine the sugar, milk, oil, eggs, poppy seeds and flavorings in a bowl and mix well. Stir in the flour mixture. Spoon the batter into three 5×9-inch loaf pans sprayed with nonstick cooking spray. Bake at 350 degrees for 1 hour. Cool in pans for 10 minutes. Remove to a wire rack to cool completely.

FOR THE TOPPING, combine the sugar, orange juice and flavorings in a bowl and mix well. Drizzle over the loaves.

Makes 3 loaves

TOPPING

3/4 cup sugar

1/4 cup orange juice

1/2 teaspoon vanilla
  extract

1/2 teaspoon almond
  extract

1/2 teaspoon butter
  flavoring

* *

Pumpkin Bread

3 1/2 cups flour

2 1/2 cups sugar

2 (4-ounce) packages
  coconut cream instant
  pudding mix

2 teaspoons baking soda

1 tablespoon pumpkin pie
  spice

1 1/2 teaspoons salt

1/8 teaspoon freshly grated
  nutmeg (optional)

1 (16-ounce) can pumpkin

1 cup vegetable oil

1/3 cup water

4 eggs

1 cup chopped pecans
  (optional)

Sift the flour, sugar, pudding mix, baking soda, pumpkin pie spice, salt and nutmeg into a bowl and mix well. Combine the pumpkin, oil, water and eggs in a bowl and mix well. Stir the pumpkin mixture into the flour mixture. Fold in the pecans.

Spoon the batter into 2 greased and floured 5×9-inch loaf pans or 8 miniature loaf pans. Bake at 325 degrees for 70 to 80 minutes or until a wooden pick inserted in the center comes out clean.

Makes 2 large loaves or 8 miniature loaves

Whole Wheat Bread

3/4 cup milk

1/3 cup margarine

1/3 cup molasses

2 tablespoons sugar

1 tablespoon salt

1 1/2 cups lukewarm water

2 envelopes dry yeast, or
 2 cakes yeast

3 1/2 cups whole wheat flour

3 3/4 cups all-purpose flour

Scald the milk in a saucepan. Add the margarine, molasses, sugar and salt and mix until blended. Let stand until lukewarm. Pour the lukewarm water into a large heated mixing bowl. Sprinkle with the yeast and stir until the yeast dissolves. Stir the lukewarm milk mixture, 2 cups of the whole wheat flour and 2 cups of the all-purpose flour into the yeast mixture. Beat until smooth. Add enough of the remaining whole wheat flour and all-purpose flour to make a soft dough and mix well.

Knead the dough on a lightly floured surface for 8 to 10 minutes or until smooth and elastic. Place the dough in a greased bowl, turning to coat the surface. Let rise, covered, in a warm place free from drafts for 1 hour or until doubled in bulk. Punch the dough down. Divide the dough into 2 equal portions. Shape each portion into a loaf in a greased 5×9-inch loaf pan. Let rise, covered, until doubled in size. Bake at 400 degrees for 25 to 30 minutes or until light brown. Remove to a wire rack to cool.

Makes 2 loaves

* * * * * * * * * * * * * * * * * *

Applesauce Muffins

1 3/4 cups flour

1 tablespoon baking powder

1/2 teaspoon salt

1/2 cup sugar

1/2 cup (1 stick) butter,
 softened

2 eggs

3/4 cup applesauce

1/4 cup (1/2 stick) butter,
 melted

1/2 cup sugar

1/4 teaspoon cinnamon

Mix the flour, baking powder and salt together. Beat 1/2 cup sugar and 1/2 cup butter in a mixing bowl until creamy. Add the eggs 1 at a time, beating well after each addition. Beat in the applesauce. Add the dry ingredients and stir just until moistened.

Fill greased muffin cups 2/3 full. Bake at 425 degrees for 15 minutes. Dip the warm muffins in 1/4 cup melted butter and then in a mixture of 1/2 cup sugar and cinnamon. Serve warm.

Makes 1 dozen muffins

Chocolate Banana Chocolate Chip Muffins

1 1/4 cups flour
1/2 cup sugar
1 tablespoon baking powder
1 teaspoon cinnamon
1/4 cup (1/2 stick) butter

6 tablespoons baking cocoa
1/4 cup hot water
2/3 cup milk
1 egg

1 teaspoon vanilla extract
2 bananas, mashed
2/3 cup semisweet mini
  chocolate chips

Sift the flour, sugar, baking powder and cinnamon into a bowl and mix well. Place the butter in a microwave-safe dish. Microwave until melted. Add the baking cocoa and hot water to the melted butter and mix well. Let stand until cool.

Whisk the milk, egg and vanilla in a bowl until blended. Stir in the bananas and baking cocoa mixture. Add the milk mixture to the flour mixture and stir just until moistened. Fold in the chocolate chips. Spoon the batter into 12 greased muffin cups or 4 dozen miniature muffin cups. Bake at 375 degrees for 22 to 25 minutes for standard muffin cups or 15 to 20 minutes for miniature muffin cups or until the muffins spring back when lightly pressed with a finger. Remove to a wire rack to cool.

Makes 1 dozen standard muffins or 4 dozen miniature muffins

Contributed by Maple Place Bed & Breakfast

* *

Four-Chippers

2 cups flour
1/2 cup packed brown sugar
2 teaspoons baking powder
2/3 cup milk

1/2 cup (1 stick) butter, melted
2 eggs
1 teaspoon vanilla extract
1/2 cup white chocolate chips

1/2 cup semisweet chocolate
  chips
1/2 cup butterscotch chips
1/2 cup peanut butter chips

Combine the flour, brown sugar and baking powder in a bowl and mix well. Whisk the milk, butter, eggs and vanilla in a bowl until blended. Add the milk mixture to the flour mixture and stir just until moistened. Fold in the chips. Fill greased muffin cups 2/3 full. Bake at 350 degrees for 15 to 20 minutes for standard muffin cups or 20 to 25 minutes for jumbo muffin cups. Remove to a wire rack to cool.

Makes 11 standard muffins or 5 jumbo muffins

Contributed by Maple Place Bed & Breakfast

Peach Muffins

1 1/2 cups plus 1 tablespoon flour

1 cup sugar

1 1/2 teaspoons cinnamon

1/2 teaspoon salt

1/2 teaspoon baking soda

1 cup fresh or canned sliced peaches, chopped

1/2 cup plus 2 tablespoons vegetable oil

2 eggs, beaten

1/2 cup chopped pecans

Combine the flour, sugar, cinnamon, salt and baking soda in a bowl and mix well. Mix the peaches, oil and eggs in a bowl. Add the peach mixture to the flour mixture and stir just until moistened. Fold in the pecans.

Fill greased muffin cups 2/3 full. Bake at 350 degrees for 25 minutes or until a wooden pick inserted in the center comes out clean. Cool on wire rack for 10 minutes.

Makes 1 dozen muffins

* *

Raspberry Muffins

1 1/2 cups flour

1 cup sugar

1 1/2 teaspoons cinnamon

1/2 teaspoon baking soda

1/2 teaspoon salt

1 (12-ounce) package frozen unsweetened raspberries, thawed

2 eggs, beaten

2/3 cup vegetable oil

1/2 cup chopped pecans

Combine the flour, sugar, cinnamon, baking soda and salt in a bowl and mix well. Make a well in the center of the flour mixture. Add the undrained raspberries and eggs to the well and stir to mix. Stir in the oil and pecans.

Spoon the batter into lightly greased muffin cups. The muffin cups will be full; the batter is heavy and will not overflow. Bake at 400 degrees for 15 to 20 minutes or until the muffins test done. Cool in pan for 5 minutes. Remove to a wire rack to cool completely. May bake in a greased and floured 5x9-inch loaf pan at 350 degrees for 1 hour or until a wooden pick inserted in the center comes out clean.

Makes 1 dozen muffins or 1 loaf

Puffed Pancake

1 cup milk

1 cup flour

1/2 cup sugar

1/4 cup orange juice

6 eggs

1/4 teaspoon salt

1/2 cup (1 stick) margarine

Maple syrup

Combine the milk, flour, sugar, orange juice, eggs and salt in a blender container or large bowl. Process until blended. Place the margarine in a 9×13-inch baking dish. Heat at 425 degrees until the margarine sizzles; do not brown.

Pour the batter over the sizzling margarine. Place the pan on the middle oven rack. Bake at 425 degrees for 20 minutes or until puffed and brown. Serve immediately with warm maple syrup.

Serves 4 to 6

* *

Southwestern Sweet Potato Cakes

2 sweet potatoes, peeled, coarsely grated

1 cup evaporated milk

1/2 cup pecan pieces, toasted

1/2 cup chopped fresh cilantro

2 eggs, beaten

1/2 teaspoon cumin

1 1/2 cups flour

Olive oil or butter

Combine the sweet potatoes, evaporated milk, pecans, cilantro, eggs and cumin in a bowl and mix well. Add the flour and stir just until moistened.

Heat a small amount of olive oil or butter in a large skillet over medium heat. Place a spoonful of the batter in the hot skillet and press flat to make a pancake approximately 4 inches in diameter. Add a second spoonful of batter and press flat. Cook for about 4 minutes on each side, turning once. Remove the pancakes to a heated platter. Repeat the process with the remaining batter.

Makes 8 pancakes

Contributed by Mimi Rippee

Focaccia

3 1/2 cups unbleached flour
2 envelopes dry yeast
2 teaspoons sugar
1 1/2 teaspoons salt
1 1/2 cups hot (120 to
    130 degrees) water

1/3 cup olive oil
1/4 cup olive oil
3 tablespoons minced fresh
    rosemary, or 1 1/2
    tablespoons dried
    rosemary

2 teaspoons minced garlic
Cornmeal
1 1/2 teaspoons coarse
    kosher salt

Combine the flour, yeast, sugar and 1 1/2 teaspoons salt in a large bowl and mix well. Combine the hot water and 1/3 cup olive oil in a 2-cup measuring cup. Check the temperature of the water with a meat thermometer to insure accuracy. Add the olive oil mixture gradually to the flour mixture, stirring constantly until a sticky dough forms. May mix at low speed with an electric mixer.

Knead the dough on a lightly floured surface until smooth and elastic, adding additional flour as needed. Place the dough in a greased bowl, turning to coat the surface. Let rise, covered with plastic wrap and a tea towel, for 45 minutes or until doubled in bulk.

Combine 1/4 cup olive oil, rosemary and garlic in a bowl and mix well. Spray a large round baking sheet with nonstick cooking spray and sprinkle lightly with cornmeal. Punch the dough down. Let rest for 5 minutes. Place the dough on the prepared baking sheet. Roll the dough into a 12-inch round with a floured rolling pin. Build up the edge of the round slightly to form a rim. Let rise, covered with plastic wrap and a tea towel, for 30 minutes.

Pierce the surface of the round with a fork. Bake at 375 degrees for 20 minutes. Drizzle with the rosemary mixture and sprinkle with 1 1/2 teaspoons kosher salt. Bake for 10 minutes longer or until light brown on the top and side. Cool on baking sheet for 5 minutes. Cut into wedges and serve with extra-virgin olive oil and fresh cracked black pepper. This bread can be shaped into a heart for Valentine's Day or a Christmas tree for the holidays.

Serves 10 to 12

Cinnamon Rolls

ROLLS

2 envelopes dry yeast

1/2 cup lukewarm water

1/2 cup sugar

2 eggs

2 teaspoons salt

1 1/4 cups milk

2 teaspoons vinegar

1/2 cup (1 stick)
margarine, melted

5 1/2 cups (about) flour

2 teaspoons baking
powder

1/4 cup (1/2 stick)
margarine, melted

1/2 cup sugar

1 tablespoon cinnamon

FOR THE ROLLS, dissolve the yeast in the lukewarm water in a bowl and mix well. Beat 1/2 cup sugar, eggs and salt in a mixing bowl until blended. Stir in a mixture of the milk and vinegar. Add 1/2 cup margarine and the yeast mixture and mix well. Stir in a mixture of 2 1/2 cups of the flour and baking powder. Add the remaining 3 cups of flour gradually and knead; may not need all 3 cups. The dough should be as sticky as possible but still manageable.

Lay a 9×13-inch piece of plastic wrap on a hard surface and sprinkle lightly with flour. Roll the dough into a rectangle on the plastic wrap. Brush the rectangle with 1/4 cup margarine and sprinkle with a mixture of 1/2 cup sugar and cinnamon. Roll as for a jelly roll and cut into 12 slices. Arrange the slices cut side up in a greased 9×13-inch baking dish. Let rise for 3 to 4 hours. Bake at 375 degrees for 20 to 25 minutes or until light brown.

FOR THE ICING, whisk the margarine, milk and vanilla in a bowl. Add the confectioners' sugar and mix until of a spreading consistency. Spread the icing over the hot rolls.

Makes 1 dozen large rolls

ICING

1/4 cup (1/2 stick)
margarine, melted

1/4 cup milk

1 teaspoon vanilla extract

2 1/2 cups confectioners'
sugar

Mom's Homemade Hot Rolls

1 envelope dry yeast	1 teaspoon salt	1/2 cup sugar
3 tablespoons lukewarm water	1 cup boiling water	4 cups flour
1/2 cup (1 stick) margarine	2 eggs	Margarine, softened

Dissolve the yeast in the lukewarm water in a small bowl. Mix 1/2 cup margarine, salt and boiling water in a heatproof bowl. Cool to lukewarm. Beat the eggs in a mixing bowl until blended. Add the yeast mixture, water mixture and sugar and beat until mixed. Add 2 cups of the flour and beat until blended. Add the remaining 2 cups flour gradually, beating constantly until smooth. Chill, covered, for 8 to 10 hours.

Divide the dough into 2 equal portions 31/2 hours before serving. Roll each portion into a round on a lightly floured surface. Spread each round with softened margarine. Cut each round into 16 equal wedges. Roll up the wedges from the wide ends. Arrange on a greased baking sheet. Let rise for 3 hours. Bake at 375 degrees for 8 to 10 minutes or until light brown.

Makes 32 rolls

* *

Oatmeal Dinner Rolls

2 cups water	1/3 cup warm (110 to	1 tablespoon sugar
1 cup quick-cooking oats	115 degrees) water	11/2 teaspoons salt
3 tablespoons butter	1/3 cup packed brown sugar	43/4 to 51/4 cups flour
1 envelope dry yeast		

Bring 2 cups water to a boil in a saucepan. Stir in the oats and butter. Cook for 1 minute, stirring constantly. Remove from heat. Cool to lukewarm. Dissolve the yeast in the warm water in a mixing bowl. Add the oat mixture, brown sugar, sugar, salt and 4 cups of the flour. Beat until smooth. Add enough of the remaining flour to make a soft dough and mix well. Knead the dough on a lightly floured surface for 6 to 8 minutes or until smooth and elastic. Place the dough in a greased bowl, turning to coat the surface.

Let rise, covered, for 1 hour or until doubled in bulk. Punch the dough down. Let rest for 10 minutes. Shape into 18 balls. Place the balls in 2 greased 9-inch round baking pans. Let rise, covered, for 45 minutes or until doubled in bulk. Bake at 350 degrees for 20 to 25 minutes or until golden brown.

Makes 18 rolls

Pull-Aparts

2 (16-ounce) loaves frozen
  bread dough
1 cup packed brown sugar
1 (6-ounce) package vanilla
  pudding and pie
  filling mix

1/2 cup (1 stick) butter,
  melted
2 tablespoons milk
2 teaspoons cinnamon
1/2 (1-pound) package
  confectioners' sugar

1/4 cup milk
2 to 3 tablespoons butter,
  melted
1 teaspoon vanilla extract

Spray 2 glass dishes with nonstick cooking spray. Place 1 bread loaf in each dish. Spray plastic wrap with nonstick cooking spray and loosely cover each loaf. Let rise for 8 to 10 hours. Pinch 1 loaf of dough into small pieces and arrange in the bottom of a greased 9×13-inch baking pan.

Combine the brown sugar, pudding mix, 1/2 cup butter, 2 tablespoons milk and cinnamon in a bowl and mix well. Drizzle the brown sugar mixture over the bread pieces. Pinch the remaining bread loaf into small pieces and place over the prepared layers. Bake at 350 degrees for 25 minutes.

Combine the confectioners' sugar, 1/4 cup milk and 2 to 3 tablespoons butter in a bowl and mix until of a spreading consistency. Stir in the vanilla. Spread over the baked layer.

Serves 12 to 15

* * * * * * * * * * * * * * * * * * * *

Breakfast Bread

Cut the biscuits from 1 can of flaky Grands biscuits into eighths. Combine the biscuit pieces, 8 beaten eggs, 1 pound crumbled crisp-cooked bacon, one 4-ounce can chopped green chiles and 2 cups shredded Cheddar cheese in a bowl and mix gently. Spoon the biscuit mixture into a greased tube or bundt pan. Bake at 350 degrees for 40 minutes. Run a knife around the outer edge of the pan and invert onto a serving platter. Slice and serve plain or topped with syrup.

Bread Baking Guide

The pleasure of baking homemade bread is matched only by eating it, except when something goes wrong. Most problems can be identified and easily avoided the next time.

Problem . . .	Cause . . .
Bread or biscuits are dry	Too much flour; too slow baking; overhandling
Bread has too-open texture or uneven texture	Too much liquid; overhandling in kneading
Strong yeast smell from baked bread	Too much yeast; overrising
Tiny white spots on crust	Too-rapid rising; dough not covered properly while rising
Crust has bad color	Too much flour used in shaping
Small flat loaves	Old yeast; not enough rising or rising much too long; oven temperature too high
Heavy compact texture	Too much flour worked into bread when kneading; insufficient rising time; oven temperature too high
Coarse texture	Too little kneading
Crumbly texture	Too much flour; undermixing; oven temperature too low
Yeasty sour flavor	Too little yeast; rising time too long
Fallen center	Rising time too long
Irregular shape	Poor technique in shaping
Surface browns too quickly	Oven temperature too high
Bread rises too long during baking and is porous in center and upper portion of loaf	Oven temperature too low

Sweets

Graham Cracker Tidbits

2 dozen graham crackers
1/2 cup packed brown sugar

1/2 cup (1 stick) margarine
1 teaspoon vanilla extract

1/2 cup chopped pecans

Arrange the graham crackers in a single layer on a baking sheet. Combine the brown sugar, margarine and vanilla in a saucepan. Bring to a boil, stirring occasionally. Boil for 1 minute. Stir in the pecans. Drizzle the brown sugar mixture over the graham crackers. Break into pieces.

Makes 2 dozen

* * * * * * * * * * * * * * * * * * *

Chocolate Chip Cheesecake

1 1/2 cups crushed chocolate
    sandwich cookies
    (about 18 cookies)
1/4 cup (1/2 stick) butter or
    margarine, melted

24 ounces cream cheese,
    softened
1 (14-ounce) can sweetened
    condensed milk

3 eggs
1 teaspoon vanilla extract
1 cup mini chocolate chips
1 teaspoon flour

Toss the cookie crumbs and butter in a bowl until coated. Pat the crumb mixture over the bottom of a springform pan.

Beat the cream cheese in a mixing bowl until light and fluffy. Add the condensed milk and beat until smooth. Beat in the eggs and vanilla until blended. Toss 1/2 cup of the chocolate chips and flour in a bowl until coated. Stir the coated chocolate chips into the cream cheese mixture.

Spoon the cream cheese mixture into the prepared pan. Sprinkle with the remaining 1/2 cup chocolate chips. Bake at 300 degrees for 1 hour or until the cheesecake springs back when lightly touched. Cool to room temperature. Chill, covered, until serving time.

Serves 10 to 12

New York Cheesecake

1/2 cup graham cracker crumbs

2 pounds cream cheese, softened

1 1/2 to 1 3/4 cups sugar

Grated zest and juice of 1 lemon (at least 3 tablespoons)

1 teaspoon vanilla extract

4 eggs

Fresh berries (optional)

Sprinkle the graham cracker crumbs over the bottom and up the side of a buttered 8-inch springform pan. Tap the bottom of the pan to discard the excess crumbs.

Combine the cream cheese, desired amount of sugar, lemon zest, lemon juice and vanilla in a mixing bowl. Beat at low speed, adding the eggs gradually. Increase the speed to high as the ingredients blend. Continue beating until the mixture is smooth. Spoon the batter into the prepared pan and shake gently to level the mixture.

Place the pan in a slightly larger baking pan. Add boiling water to the larger pan to a depth of 1/2 inch. Bake at 250 degrees for 1 1/2 hours. Increase the oven temperature to 275 degrees. Bake for 30 minutes longer. Turn off the oven. Let stand in the oven with the door closed for 1 hour.

Lift the cheesecake out of the water bath and place on a wire rack. Let stand for 2 hours. Chill, covered, in the refrigerator. Top each serving with fresh berries.

Serves 10 to 12

* *

Blackberry Cobbler

1 to 1 1/2 quarts fresh or frozen blackberries

2 cups (about) sugar

6 tablespoons cornstarch, or 1/2 cup flour

2 refrigerator pie pastries

2 tablespoons butter or margarine

Combine the blackberries, sugar and cornstarch in a bowl and mix gently. Taste and add additional sugar if desired. Let stand at room temperature for 20 minutes. If using frozen berries, thaw and combine undrained berries with the sugar mixture.

Fit 1 of the pie pastries in a 10-inch deep-dish pie plate. Spoon the berry mixture into the prepared pie plate and dot with the butter. Top with the remaining pie pastry, sealing the edge and cutting vents. Bake at 400 degrees for 45 minutes or until golden brown.

Serves 6 to 8

Southern Bread Pudding

BREAD PUDDING

10 slices French bread, lightly toasted

1/2 cup golden raisins

1 1/2 cups sugar

8 eggs, lightly beaten

3 cups milk, scalded

3 cups heavy cream, scalded

1 tablespoon vanilla extract

1/4 teaspoon salt

1 1/2 teaspoons cinnamon

For the bread pudding, arrange the bread in a baking dish. Sprinkle with the raisins. Beat the sugar and eggs in a mixing bowl until blended. Add the milk and heavy cream gradually, beating constantly until mixed. Stir in the vanilla and salt.

Pour the egg mixture over the bread. Sprinkle with the cinnamon. Bake at 350 degrees for 30 to 40 minutes or until set. Serve hot or chilled.

For the sauce, combine the sugar, cream and butter in a small saucepan. Cook over medium heat for 5 to 15 minutes or until of a sauce consistency,

BUTTER CREAM SAUCE

1 cup sugar

1/2 cup cream or half-and-half

1/3 cup butter

1/2 teaspoon vanilla extract

1/8 teaspoon nutmeg

stirring occasionally. Stir in the vanilla and nutmeg. Spoon some of the sauce over each serving of bread pudding. If time is of the essence, top each serving with whipped cream instead of the sauce.

Serves 8

* * * * * * * * * * * * * * * * * * *

Praline Sauce

Combine 1 cup packed brown sugar, 1/4 cup corn syrup and 2 tablespoons butter in a saucepan. Cook over low heat until blended, stirring frequently. Stir in 1/2 cup half-and-half. Add 1 cup chopped toasted pecans and 1 1/4 teaspoons vanilla extract. Cook until thickened and heated through, stirring frequently. Serve warm or cold over cheesecake or ice cream.

Ultimate Banana Pudding

1 (4-ounce) package vanilla
   instant pudding mix
2 cups skim milk
1 cup plain low-fat yogurt

1 (14-ounce) can sweetened
   condensed milk
4 ounces whipped topping
1 teaspoon vanilla extract

1 (12-ounce) package
   vanilla wafers
2 pounds bananas, sliced

Combine the pudding mix and skim milk in a bowl. Prepare the pudding using package directions. Add the yogurt, condensed milk, whipped topping and vanilla to the pudding and mix until smooth.

Reserve 10 to 12 vanilla wafers. Layer the remaining vanilla wafers, bananas and pudding mixture in a 9×13-inch dish until all of the ingredients are used, ending with the pudding. Crush the reserved vanilla wafers and sprinkle over the top of the prepared layers. Chill, covered, for 8 to 10 hours.

Serves 12

* *

Creamy Gelatin Surprise

2 1/2 cups pretzel sticks,
   broken
3/4 cup (1 1/2 sticks)
   margarine, melted
3 tablespoons sugar

8 ounces cream cheese,
   softened
1 cup confectioners' sugar
8 ounces whipped topping
2 1/2 cups water

1 (6-ounce) package
   raspberry gelatin
2 (10-ounce) packages
   frozen raspberries

Combine the pretzels, margarine and sugar in a bowl and mix well. Spread the pretzel mixture over the bottom of a 9×13-inch baking pan. Bake at 350 degrees for 10 minutes. Let stand until cool.

Beat the cream cheese and confectioners' sugar in a mixing bowl until smooth. Fold in the whipped topping. Spread over the baked layer.

Bring the water to a boil in a saucepan. Remove from heat. Add the gelatin and stir until dissolved. Stir in the frozen raspberries. Return the mixture to a boil, stirring occasionally. Chill until partially set but still pourable. Pour the gelatin mixture over the prepared layers. Chill, covered, for 2 hours or until set. Cut into squares before serving.

Serves 15

Strawberry Tiramisu

6 eggs	4 1/2 cups mascarpone cheese	Fresh strawberries, thinly
1 cup sugar	Ladyfingers or sliced pound	sliced
1/2 cup brandy	cake	Whipped cream (optional)

Combine the eggs and sugar in a double boiler. Cook until the mixture triples in volume and a thermometer registers 160 degrees for 6 minutes, beating constantly with a mixer. Remove bowl from the water. Add the brandy 1 tablespoon at a time, beating well after each addition. Continue beating the custard for 5 minutes or until cool. Add the mascarpone cheese gradually, beating constantly until smooth. Chill, covered, for 30 minutes or until cold.

Cover the bottom of a 9x11-inch dish sprayed with nonstick cooking spray with ladyfingers. Spread with 1/3 of the custard and top with strawberries. Repeat the layering process until all of the custard is used, ending with strawberries. Garnish each serving with a dollop of whipped cream.

Make your own mascarpone cheese by blending 1 1/2 pounds cream cheese, 3/4 cup heavy whipping cream and 7 1/2 tablespoons sour cream.

Serves 15

* *

On September 17, 1893, the day after the Cherokee Strip Land Run, Baptist homesteaders met in Enid for the first time to worship. On January 7, 1894, the First Baptist Church of Enid was formed. Regular meetings were held in a room on the west side of the square that formerly housed a saloon. The first brick building on the corner of Maine and Adams was built in 1908. First Baptist Church continues today at the same location.

Cappuccino Frozen Delight

1 package chocolate sandwich cookies, crushed

$1/2$ to $3/4$ cup (1 to $1^1/2$ sticks) butter or margarine, melted

$1/2$ gallon coffee ice cream, softened

1 (16-ounce) jar hot fudge topping

$1^1/2$ cups whipping cream

3 tablespoons Kahlúa

Reserve $3/4$ cup of the cookie crumbs. Combine the remaining cookie crumbs and butter in a bowl and mix well. Press the crumb mixture over the bottom of a 9×13-inch dish. Spread with the ice cream and drizzle with the fudge topping. Freeze, covered, for 30 minutes.

Beat the whipping cream in a mixing bowl until stiff peaks form. Fold in the Kahlúa. Spread the whipped cream mixture over the prepared layers. Sprinkle with the reserved cookie crumbs. Freeze, covered, for 8 hours or until firm.

For a children's variation, substitute vanilla ice cream for the coffee ice cream, substitute chocolate syrup for the hot fudge topping and top with whipped topping, omitting the Kahlúa.

Serves 15 to 20

* *

Chocolate Tortoni

8 ounces German's sweet chocolate, or 1 cup semisweet chocolate chips

$2/3$ cup light or dark corn syrup

2 cups whipping cream

$1^1/2$ cups chocolate sandwich cookie crumbs

1 cup walnuts or pecans, chopped

Combine the chocolate and corn syrup in a microwave-safe dish. Microwave on High for 1 minute and stir. Add $1/2$ cup of the whipping cream and mix well. Chill for 15 minutes or until cool.

Beat the remaining $1^1/2$ cups whipping cream in a mixing bowl until soft peaks form. Fold the whipped cream into the chocolate mixture. Stir in the cookie crumbs and walnuts. Spoon the chocolate mixture into muffin cups lined with silver baking cups. Freeze for 4 to 6 hours or until firm. Garnish as desired.

Makes 1 to $1^1/2$ dozen

Fruit Wagon Wheel

SUGAR COOKIE CRUST

2 1/2 cups flour

1 teaspoon baking soda

1 teaspoon cream of tartar

1 1/2 cups confectioners'
sugar

1 cup (2 sticks) butter,
softened

2 teaspoons vanilla
extract

1 teaspoon almond
extract

1 egg

FOR THE CRUST, mix the flour, baking soda and cream of tartar together. Combine the confectioners' sugar, butter, flavorings and egg in a mixing bowl and beat until smooth. Stir in the dry ingredients. Chill, covered, for 2 hours.

Roll or pat the dough over the bottom and up the side of a round baking pan or over the bottom of a 9×13-inch baking pan. Pierce the dough with a fork. Bake at 375 degrees for 20 minutes or until light brown. Let stand until cool.

FOR THE TOPPING, beat the cream cheese, sugar, orange zest and milk in a mixing bowl until creamy. Spread the cream cheese mixture evenly over the baked layer. Chill, covered, in the refrigerator. Top with the desired fresh fruit.

FOR THE GLAZE, combine the sugar and cornstarch in a saucepan and mix well. Stir in the orange juice, water, orange zest, lemon zest, lemon juice and salt. Cook until of a drizzling consistency, stirring constantly. Remove from heat. Let stand until cool. Drizzle over the top.

Serves 12 to 15

CREAMY ORANGE TOPPING

8 ounces cream cheese,
softened

1/3 cup sugar

3 tablespoons grated
orange zest

1 tablespoon milk

Assorted sliced fresh fruits
such as kiwifruit,
grapes, bananas,
strawberries and
blueberries

CITRUS GLAZE

1 cup sugar

3 tablespoons cornstarch

1 cup orange juice

3/4 cup water

1 teaspoon grated
orange zest

1 teaspoon grated
lemon zest

1/2 teaspoon lemon juice

Salt to taste

Raspberry Almond Tart

CRUST
1/2 cup (1 stick) margarine, softened
1/2 cup sugar
1 egg
1 1/2 cups flour
1 cup slivered almonds, finely chopped
1 teaspoon almond extract

FOR THE CRUST, beat the margarine and sugar in a mixing bowl until creamy. Add the egg. Beat at medium speed until blended. Add the flour, almonds and flavoring. Beat at medium speed until a soft dough forms, scraping the bowl frequently.

Pat the dough over the bottom and 2/3 of the way up the side of a 10-inch springform pan. Chill for 45 minutes.

FOR THE FILLING, beat the cream cheese, confectioners' sugar, eggs, lemon juice and flavoring in a mixing bowl until creamy. Spread over the chilled layer. Bake at 325 degrees for 25 minutes. Let stand until cool.

FOR THE TOPPING, combine the sugar and cornstarch in a saucepan and mix well. Stir in the raspberries. Cook over low heat until thickened, stirring constantly. Bring to a boil. Boil for 1 minute. Remove from heat. Let stand until cool. Spoon the raspberry topping over the prepared layers. Chill, covered, until serving time.

Serves 12

CREAM CHEESE FILLING
8 ounces cream cheese, softened
3/4 cup confectioners' sugar
2 eggs
2 teaspoons lemon juice
1/2 teaspoon almond extract

RASPBERRY TOPPING
3/4 cup sugar
2 1/2 tablespoons cornstarch
5 cups frozen red raspberries

Warm Apple Cake with Vanilla Cream Sauce

APPLE CAKE

2 1/2 cups flour

2 teaspoons baking powder

1 teaspoon baking soda

2 cups sugar

1 cup vegetable oil

2 eggs

1 teaspoon vanilla extract

3 cups chopped apples

1/2 cup chopped walnuts

1/3 cup packed brown
  sugar

1 teaspoon cinnamon

VANILLA CREAM SAUCE

1 cup sugar

2 tablespoons flour

1 1/2 cups whipping cream

1/2 cup (1 stick) butter

2 teaspoons vanilla extract

FOR THE CAKE, mix the flour, baking powder and baking soda. Combine the sugar, oil, eggs and vanilla in a mixing bowl. Beat until blended. Add the dry ingredients and beat until smooth. Stir in the apples; the batter will be stiff.

Spoon the batter into a greased 9×13-inch baking dish. Mix the walnuts, brown sugar and cinnamon in a bowl. Sprinkle the walnut mixture over the top. Bake at 350 degrees for 40 to 50 minutes or until the cake tests done.

FOR THE SAUCE, combine the sugar and flour in a saucepan and mix well. Add the whipping cream, butter and vanilla. Cook over medium heat until the butter melts, stirring frequently. Bring to a boil, whisking constantly until thickened. Remove from heat. Stir in the vanilla. Spoon the sauce over the warm cake.

Serves 15

Contributed by Maple Place Bed & Breakfast

Nut Knowledge

★ *Nuts in the shell stay fresh longer than shelled nuts.*

★ *Store shelled nuts in airtight containers to keep from becoming rancid.*

★ *Grinding nuts in a blender produces more oil. For drier nuts, use a nut grinder.*

★ *Nuts are more easily sliced and shredded when warm.*

★ *To keep nuts from sinking in batter, heat them in the oven before adding.*

★ *To blanche and skin, soak in boiling water until the skins wrinkle.*

Carrot Cake

CARROT CAKE

2 cups sifted flour

2 teaspoons baking soda

2 teaspoons cinnamon

1 teaspoon salt

1/2 teaspoon nutmeg

1/2 teaspoon ginger

2 cups sugar

1 cup vegetable or
canola oil

4 eggs

3 cups grated carrots

*F*OR THE CAKE, combine the flour, baking soda, cinnamon, salt, nutmeg and ginger in a bowl and mix well. Beat the sugar and oil in a mixing bowl until blended. Add the eggs 1 at a time, mixing well after each addition. Beat in the flour mixture until blended. Stir in the carrots.

Spoon the batter into 2 greased and floured 9-inch round cake pans. Bake at 350 degrees for 30 to 35 minutes or until the layers test done. Cool in pans for 10 minutes. Remove to a wire rack to cool completely.

CREAM CHEESE FROSTING

8 ounces cream cheese,
softened

1/2 cup (1 stick)
margarine, softened

1 teaspoon vanilla extract

1 (1-pound) package
confectioners' sugar

1/2 cup chopped pecans

FOR THE FROSTING, beat the cream cheese, margarine and vanilla in a mixing bowl until creamy. Add the confectioners' sugar. Beat until of a spreading consistency, scraping the bowl occasionally. Stir in the pecans. Spread the frosting between the layers and over the top and side of the cake.

Serves 12

* * * * * * * * * * * * * * * * * * * *

Heavenly Icing

Combine 1 cup milk and 3 tablespoons flour in a jar with a tight-fitting lid and seal tightly. Shake to mix. Pour the milk mixture into a saucepan. Bring to a boil, stirring constantly; reduce heat. Simmer for 1 minute or until thickened, stirring constantly. Let stand until cool or chill. Beat 1 cup sugar and 1 cup softened butter in a mixing bowl until creamy. Stir in 1 teaspoon vanilla extract. Add the milk mixture to the creamed mixture and beat until of the consistency of whipped cream. Spread the icing over your favorite cake. Chill until serving time.

Granny's Chocolate Cake

2 cups chocolate syrup
2 (7-ounce) chocolate bars,
    broken
2 cups sugar

1 cup (2 sticks) butter,
    softened
4 eggs
1 cup buttermilk

1/2 teaspoon baking soda
2 2/3 cups flour, sifted
1 1/2 teaspoons vanilla
    extract

Combine the chocolate syrup and chocolate bars in a saucepan. Cook over low heat until blended, stirring frequently. Remove from heat. Let stand until cool.

Beat the sugar and butter in a mixing bowl until creamy. Add the eggs 1 at a time, mixing well after each addition. Stir in the chocolate mixture. Combine the buttermilk and baking soda in a 2-cup measuring cup and stir until foamy. Add the buttermilk mixture and flour alternately, beating well after each addition. Stir in the vanilla. Spoon the batter into a greased bundt pan. Bake at 350 degrees for 1 hour.

Serves 16

* *

Chocolate Chip Cake

1/2 cup sugar
1 teaspoon cinnamon
2 cups flour
1 1/2 cups sugar

1 1/3 cups sour cream
2/3 cup margarine, softened
3 eggs
1 teaspoon baking powder

1 teaspoon vanilla extract
1/2 teaspoon baking soda
2 cups semisweet chocolate
    chips

Combine 1/2 cup sugar and cinnamon in a bowl and mix well. Combine the flour, 1 1/2 cups sugar, sour cream, margarine, eggs, baking powder, vanilla and baking soda in a mixing bowl. Beat for 4 minutes, scraping the bowl occasionally.

Layer the batter, cinnamon mixture and chocolate chips 1/2 at a time in a greased 9×13-inch cake pan. Bake at 350 degrees for 30 to 35 minutes or until a wooden pick inserted in the center comes out clean. Cool in pan on a wire rack.

Serves 15

Chocolate Chocolate Chip Cake

1 (2-layer) package devil's
food cake mix
1 cup sour cream
3/4 cup water

1 (4-ounce) package
chocolate instant
pudding mix
1/2 cup vegetable oil

4 eggs
1 cup chocolate chips
Chocolate syrup

Combine the cake mix, sour cream, water, pudding mix, oil and eggs in a mixing bowl. Beat until smooth, scraping the bowl occasionally. Fold in the chocolate chips.

Spoon the batter into a greased and floured tube pan. Bake at 350 degrees for 45 to 60 minutes or until the cake tests done. Cool in pan until the cake edge separates from the side of the pan. Invert onto a cake plate and drizzle the warm cake with chocolate syrup.

Serves 12

*　*　*　*　*　*　*　*　*　*　*　*　*　*　*　*　*　*　*　*

Chocolate Fudge Sheet Cake

2 cups each sugar and flour
1 teaspoon baking soda
1/2 teaspoon salt
1 cup sour cream
1/2 cup buttermilk
2 eggs, lightly beaten

1 cup (2 sticks) butter or
margarine
1 cup water
1/4 cup baking cocoa
1/2 cup (1 stick) butter or
margarine

1/3 cup milk
1/4 cup baking cocoa
1 (1-pound) package
confectioners' sugar
1 teaspoon vanilla extract

Combine the sugar, flour, baking soda and salt in a bowl and mix well. Stir in the sour cream, buttermilk and eggs. Heat 1 cup butter in a heavy saucepan over medium heat until melted. Whisk in the water and 1/4 cup baking cocoa. Bring to a boil, whisking constantly. Remove from heat. Stir the cocoa mixture into the flour mixture. Pour the batter into a lightly greased 15x19-inch sheet cake pan. Bake at 325 degrees for 25 to 30 minutes or until a wooden pick inserted in the center comes out clean.

Heat 1/2 cup butter in a saucepan over medium heat until melted. Whisk in the milk and 1/4 cup baking cocoa. Bring to a boil and remove from heat. Add the confectioners' sugar gradually, whisking constantly until smooth. Stir in the vanilla. Spread the frosting evenly over the top of the warm cake. Garnish with miniature peanut butter cup candies.

Serves 15 to 20

Superior Butternut Cake

BUTTERNUT CAKE

2 cups sugar

1 cup (2 sticks) butter, softened

4 eggs

1/8 teaspoon salt

1 cup all-purpose flour

11/2 cups self-rising flour

1 cup milk

1 tablespoon butternut flavoring

FOR THE CAKE, cream the sugar, butter, eggs and salt in a mixing bowl for 10 minutes, scraping the bowl occasionally. Beat in 1 cup all-purpose flour. Add 11/2 cups self-rising flour alternately with the milk, mixing well after each addition. Stir in the flavoring. Spoon the batter into 4 buttered and floured cake pans. Bake at 350 degrees for 25 to 30 minutes or until the layers test done. Cool in pans for 10 minutes. Remove to wire racks to cool completely.

FOR THE FROSTING, beat the cream cheese and butter in a mixing bowl until creamy. Add the confectioners' sugar gradually, beating constantly until of a spreading consistency. Stir in the flavoring. Spread the frosting between the layers and over the top and side of the cake. Pat some of the pecans around the side of the cake and sprinkle the remaining pecans over the top. For butternut flavoring, combine 1 teaspoon each butter extract, vanilla extract and almond extract.

Serves 12

BUTTERNUT FROSTING

8 ounces cream cheese, softened

1/2 cup (1 stick) butter, softened

1 (1-pound) package confectioners' sugar

1 tablespoon butternut flavoring

1 cup finely chopped pecans

* *

Warm Caramel Sauce

Heat 12 vanilla caramels and 1/2 cup whipping cream in a saucepan over medium heat until blended, stirring frequently. Add 1/4 teaspoon rum if desired and mix well. Drizzle the caramel sauce over bread pudding, ice cream or pound cake.

Not-Your-Average Fruitcake!

1 (16-ounce) can fruit
    cocktail
2 cups flour

2 teaspoons baking soda
1/2 teaspoon salt
1 1/2 cups sugar

2 eggs
1 cup packed brown sugar
1/2 cup chopped nuts

Drain the fruit cocktail, reserving 2/3 cup of the juice. Mix the flour, baking soda and salt together. Beat the sugar and eggs in a mixing bowl until creamy. Add the reserved juice and beat until blended. Add the flour mixture. Beat for 2 minutes. Fold in the fruit cocktail.

    Spoon the batter into a lightly greased 9×13-inch cake pan. Sprinkle with the brown sugar and nuts. Bake at 350 degrees for 35 to 40 minutes or until the cake tests done. Serve warm topped with ice cream or whipped cream.

    Serves 15

* *

Harvey Wallbanger Cake

CAKE
1 (2-layer) package
    orange cake mix
1 (4-ounce) package
    vanilla instant
    pudding mix
1 cup vegetable oil
3/4 cup orange juice
1/4 cup vodka
1/4 cup galliano
4 eggs

FOR THE CAKE, combine the cake mix, pudding mix, oil, orange juice, vodka, galliano and eggs in a mixing bowl. Beat for 4 minutes, scraping the bowl occasionally.

    Spoon the batter into a greased and lightly floured bundt pan. Bake at 350 degrees for 45 to 50 minutes. Cool in pan for 20 minutes. Invert onto a cake plate.

    FOR THE GLAZE, combine the confectioners' sugar, orange juice, vodka and galliano in a bowl and mix well. Drizzle over the warm cake.

    Serves 16

ORANGE GLAZE
1 cup confectioners'
    sugar
1 tablespoon orange
    juice
1 tablespoon vodka
1 tablespoon galliano

Italian Crème Cake

CAKE

2 cups sifted flour

1 teaspoon baking soda

1/2 teaspoon salt

2 cups sugar

1 cup (2 sticks)
    margarine, softened

5 egg yolks, lightly beaten

1 cup buttermilk

1 tablespoon vanilla
    extract

1 cup chopped pecans

1 cup shredded coconut

5 egg whites, stiffly beaten

For the cake, mix the flour, baking soda and salt together. Beat the sugar and margarine in a mixing bowl until creamy. Add the egg yolks and beat until smooth. Add the dry ingredients and beat until blended.

Combine the buttermilk and vanilla in a bowl and mix well. Add the buttermilk mixture and flour mixture alternately, mixing well after each addition. Stir in the pecans and coconut. Fold in the egg whites.

Spoon the batter into two 9-inch cake pans or three 8-inch cake pans. Bake at 325 degrees for 35 to 40 minutes or until the layers test done. Cool in pans for 10 minutes. Remove to a wire rack to cool completely.

CREAMY COCONUT FROSTING

8 ounces cream cheese,
    softened

1/4 cup (1/2 stick)
    margarine, softened

1 tablespoon vanilla extract

1 (1-pound) package
    confectioners' sugar

1 cup shredded coconut

3/4 cup chopped pecans

For the frosting, beat the cream cheese, margarine and vanilla in a mixing bowl until creamy. Add the confectioners' sugar gradually, beating constantly until of a spreading consistency. Reserve 1/4 cup of the coconut. Add the remaining coconut and pecans to the frosting and mix well.

Spread the frosting between the layers and over the top and side of the cake. Sprinkle the reserved coconut over the top.

Serves 12

Peanut Butter Cake

CAKE

2 cups flour

2 cups sugar

1 teaspoon baking soda

1/4 teaspoon salt

1 cup water

3/4 cup (1 1/2 sticks) butter
or margarine

1/2 cup vegetable oil

1/2 cup peanut butter

1/2 cup buttermilk

2 eggs, beaten

1 teaspoon vanilla extract

PEANUT BUTTER FROSTING

1 cup sugar

1/2 cup evaporated milk

1 tablespoon butter or
margarine

1/2 cup extra-crunchy
peanut butter

1/2 cup miniature
marshmallows

1 teaspoon vanilla extract

1/2 cup canned chocolate
frosting

FOR THE CAKE, combine the flour, sugar, baking soda and salt in a bowl and mix well. Bring the water, butter, oil and peanut butter to a boil in a saucepan, stirring frequently. Add the peanut butter mixture to the dry ingredients and mix well. Stir in the buttermilk, eggs and vanilla. Spoon the batter into a greased 11×15-inch sheet cake pan. Bake at 350 degrees for 20 minutes.

FOR THE FROSTING, combine the sugar, evaporated milk and butter in a saucepan. Bring to a boil, stirring occasionally. Boil for 2 to 3 minutes, stirring occasionally. Remove from heat. Add the peanut butter, marshmallows and vanilla and stir until blended. Spread the frosting over the warm cake. Spoon the canned frosting into a microwave-safe dish. Microwave for 20 seconds or until of a drizzling consistency. Drizzle over the cake.

TO MAKE A THREE-LAYER CAKE, bake the layers in three 8-inch cake pans. Spread the Peanut Butter Frosting between the layers and over the top. Spread your favorite cream cheese frosting over the side of the cake, substituting 1/4 cup of the margarine with peanut butter.

Serves 12

Pineapple Sheet Cake

CAKE

2 cups flour

1 1/2 teaspoons baking soda

2 cups sugar

1/2 cup (1 stick) butter

2 eggs, beaten

1 teaspoon vanilla extract

1 (20-ounce) can pineapple

1 cup chopped nuts

FOR THE CAKE, mix the flour and baking soda together. Beat the sugar and butter in a mixing bowl until creamy. Add the eggs and vanilla and beat until blended. Beat in the dry ingredients. Stir the undrained pineapple and nuts into the batter. Spoon the batter into a greased sheet cake pan. Bake at 350 degrees for 35 minutes.

FOR THE FROSTING, beat the cream cheese, butter and vanilla in a mixing bowl until creamy. Add the confectioners' sugar gradually, beating constantly until of a spreading consistency. Stir in the pecans. Spread the frosting over the top of the hot cake. Chill, covered, until serving time.

Serves 15 to 20

CREAM CHEESE FROSTING

8 ounces cream cheese, softened

1/2 cup (1 stick) butter, softened

1 teaspoon vanilla extract

1 3/4 cups confectioners' sugar

1/2 cup chopped pecans or walnuts

* *

Oh No! I Don't Have Any . . .

Baking powder	2 tablespoons cream of tartar, 1 teaspoon baking soda and 1 teaspoon cornstarch
Brown sugar	1/2 cup granulated sugar, 1/2 cup molasses and 1/4 teaspoon baking soda
Buttermilk	1 tablespoon vinegar or lemon juice plus 1 cup milk
Corn syrup	1 cup sugar with 1/4 cup water
Confectioners' sugar	1 cup regular sugar blended with 1 tablespoon cornstarch.
Sour cream	1 cup cottage cheese blended with 1 tablespoon milk and 1 teaspoon lemon juice
Unsweetened chocolate	3 tablespoons unsweetened cocoa plus 1 tablespoon butter or shortening

Pound Cake with Vanilla Sauce

POUND CAKE

10 1/2 ounces sifted flour

1 teaspoon baking powder

1/8 teaspoon salt

13 1/2 ounces butter

10 1/2 ounces sugar

3 ounces milk

Juice of 1/2 lemon

1 tablespoon vanilla extract

6 eggs, beaten

*F*OR THE CAKE, mix the flour, baking powder and salt together. Beat the butter and sugar in a mixing bowl for 10 minutes or until the sugar dissolves. Add the flour mixture alternately with the milk, lemon juice and vanilla, starting with dry ingredients and ending with wet ingredients and mixing well after each addition. Add the eggs 1/3 at a time, mixing well after each addition.

Spoon the batter into a buttered and floured 5×9-inch loaf pan. Bake at 350 degrees for 45 to 60 minutes or until the loaf tests done.

VANILLA SAUCE

1 cup sugar

2 tablespoons flour

1/8 teaspoon salt

2 cups water

2 teaspoons vanilla extract

3 tablespoons butter, chilled

FOR THE SAUCE, combine the sugar, flour and salt in a bowl and mix well. Bring the water and vanilla to a boil in a saucepan. Add the boiling mixture to the sugar mixture gradually, whisking constantly. Add the butter and whisk until blended. Pour the sauce over the warm cake.

Serves 12

Contributed by La Luna Blu Restaurant

Zucchini Cake

CAKE

2 cups flour

2 teaspoons baking soda

2 teaspoons cinnamon

1 teaspoon salt

1/2 teaspoon baking
    powder

2 cups sugar

1 cup vegetable oil

3 eggs, beaten

1 tablespoon vanilla
    extract

2 cups ground zucchini

FOR THE CAKE, combine the flour, baking soda, cinnamon, salt and baking powder in a bowl and mix well. Beat the sugar and oil in a mixing bowl until creamy. Beat in the eggs and vanilla until blended. Add the flour mixture and beat until smooth. Stir in the zucchini.

Spoon the batter into a greased and floured 9×13-inch cake pan. Bake at 350 degrees for 35 minutes or until a wooden pick inserted in the center comes out clean.

FOR THE GLAZE, bring the sugar, margarine, evaporated milk and vanilla to a boil in a saucepan. Boil for 2 minutes, stirring frequently. Remove from heat. Let stand until cool. Whisk the glaze until smooth. Drizzle the glaze over the cake.

Serves 15

GLAZE

1 cup sugar

6 tablespoons margarine

1/2 cup evaporated milk

1 teaspoon vanilla extract

More Flavored Butters

Prepare Basic Butter Base as directed on page 94.

*For **Citrus Butter**, add 1 tablespoon confectioners' sugar and 1/2 teaspoon finely shredded orange or lemon zest.*

Chocolate Almond Cream Confections

CHOCOLATE CONFECTIONS

1 cup slivered almonds

1/2 cup (1 stick) butter (no substitutions)

1/4 cup sugar

2 tablespoons baking cocoa

2 teaspoons vanilla extract

1 egg, lightly beaten

1/4 teaspoon salt

1 3/4 cups vanilla wafer crumbs

1/2 cup flaked coconut

CREAM FROSTING AND TOPPING

1/3 cup butter, softened

3 to 4 tablespoons milk

3 cups sifted confectioners' sugar

1/2 teaspoon vanilla extract

2 ounces semisweet baking chocolate

For the confections, spread the almonds on a baking sheet. Toast at 350 degrees for 10 minutes. Process the almonds in a miniature food processor until coarsely chopped. Combine the butter, sugar, baking cocoa, vanilla, egg and salt in a heavy saucepan. Cook over low heat until the butter melts and the mixture begins to thicken, stirring constantly. Remove from heat.

Add the almonds, vanilla wafer crumbs and coconut to the chocolate mixture and mix well with a wooden spoon. Pat the chocolate mixture into an ungreased 9×9-inch dish. Chill, covered, for 2 hours or longer.

For the frosting and topping, beat the butter in a mixing bowl until light and fluffy. Add 3 tablespoons of the milk and vanilla and beat until smooth. Add the confectioners' sugar gradually, beating constantly until smooth and adding enough of the remaining 1 tablespoon milk to make the frosting of a spreading consistency; the frosting should be stiff. Spread the frosting over the chilled layer using a rubber spatula. Chill, covered, for 2 to 10 hours.

Cut into chilled layers into thirty-six 1 1/2-inch squares. Remove the squares to a baking sheet lined with waxed paper; do not allow the squares to touch. Place the chocolate in a heavy-duty sealable plastic bag and seal tightly. Submerge the bag in hot water until the chocolate melts. Snip a tiny hole in one corner of the bag and drizzle the chocolate in a decorative pattern over the squares. Chill just until the chocolate is set. Serve cold.

Makes 3 dozen

Almond Roca Candy

4 cups slivered almonds
2 tablespoons butter
1/8 teaspoon salt

2 cups (4 sticks) butter
2 cups sugar
6 tablespoons cold water

2 tablespoons light corn syrup
2 (8-ounce) milk chocolate
   candy bars

Brown the almonds in 2 tablespoons butter in a skillet, stirring frequently. Stir in the salt. Process 1 cup of the almonds in a food processor or blender until ground.

Heat 2 cups butter in a heavy saucepan over low heat until melted. Stir in the sugar, cold water and corn syrup. Stir in the remaining slivered almonds. Bring to a boil. Boil until a candy thermometer registers 290 degrees, soft-crack stage. This is very important step; DO NOT stop short of 290 degrees or your candy will be too soft. Remove from heat.

Pour the candy mixture immediately onto a baking sheet lined with foil. This will harden quickly. Heat 1 of the chocolate bars in a double boiler until melted, stirring occasionally. Spread over the top of the candy and sprinkle with the ground almonds. Let stand at room temperature for 8 to 10 hours; do not chill. Invert the candy. Heat the remaining chocolate bar in a double boiler until melted and spread over the candy. Let stand until firm. Break into pieces and store in sealable plastic bags in the refrigerator.

Makes 4 pounds

* *

Cream Caramels

3/4 cup nut pieces
2 cups sugar
1 cup cream or evaporated
   milk

3/4 cup light corn syrup
1/2 cup (1 stick) butter or
   margarine

1 cup cream or evaporated
   milk
1 teaspoon vanilla extract

Sprinkle the nuts over the bottom of a buttered 8×8-inch pan. Bring the sugar, 1 cup cream, corn syrup and butter slowly to a boil in a saucepan, stirring occasionally. Stir in 1 cup cream.

Cook until the mixture begins to thicken, stirring frequently. Continue cooking until the mixture darkens, stirring constantly. Continue cooking to 254 degrees on a candy thermometer, hard-ball stage. Remove from heat.

Stir in the vanilla. Pour the hot mixture over the nuts. Let stand until firm. Cut into small squares.

Makes 2 pounds

Chocolate Crème de Menthe Bites

1/2 cup (1 stick) butter or margarine, melted
1/2 cup confectioners' sugar
1/2 cup baking cocoa
1 egg, beaten
1 teaspoon vanilla extract

2 cups graham cracker crumbs
3 cups confectioners' sugar
1/3 cup crème de menthe
1/2 cup (1 stick) butter or margarine, melted

1 1/2 cups semisweet chocolate chips
1/4 cup (1/2 stick) butter or margarine, melted

Combine 1/2 cup butter, 1/2 cup confectioners' sugar, baking cocoa and egg in a double boiler and mix well. Bring the water to a boil; reduce heat to low. Cook until thickened, stirring constantly. Remove from heat. Stir in the vanilla and graham cracker crumbs. Press the crumb mixture over the bottom of a greased 9×13-inch dish. Chill for 15 minutes.

Beat 3 cups confectioners' sugar, crème de menthe and 1/2 cup butter in a mixing bowl until smooth. Spread the crème de menthe mixture over the chilled layer. Chill for 1 hour. Combine the chocolate chips and 1/4 cup butter in a double boiler. Cook over low heat until smooth, stirring constantly. Spread the chocolate mixture over the prepared layers. Let stand until cool. Cut into squares. Store, covered, in the refrigerator.

Makes 8 dozen squares

* *

Less-Stress Divinity

2 cups sugar
1/2 cup water

1/3 cup light corn syrup
2 egg whites

1 teaspoon vanilla extract
1/2 cup chopped nuts

Combine the sugar, water and corn syrup in a microwave-safe bowl. Microwave on High for 3 minutes; stir. Microwave for 6 to 8 minutes longer or to 250 degrees on a candy thermometer, hardball stage.

Beat the egg whites in a mixing bowl until stiff peaks form. Add the hot syrup gradually to the egg whites, beating constantly. Add the vanilla and beat until thickened. Fold in the nuts. Drop the divinity by teaspoonfuls onto a sheet of waxed paper. Let stand until firm.

Makes 1 pound

Meringue Kisses

6 egg whites
1/8 teaspoon cream of tartar

1 (1-pound) package
confectioners' sugar

1 cup chopped pecans

Beat the egg whites in a mixing bowl until frothy. Add the cream of tartar. Beat until stiff and dry. Add the confectioners' sugar gradually, beating well after each addition. The meringue should be stiff and stand in peaks. Fold in the pecans.

Drop the meringue by teaspoonfuls onto a baking sheet. Bake at 325 degrees for 10 to 12 minutes. Remove immediately to a wire rack to cool. Omit the pecans and shape the meringue to form tart shells for variety. Bake as directed and fill with strawberries and/or vanilla ice cream.

Makes 3 to 4 dozen kisses

* *

Peanut Butter Poppers

1 (18-ounce) jar peanut
butter
1/2 cup (1 stick) butter,
softened

1 teaspoon vanilla extract
1 (1-pound) package
confectioners' sugar

Chocolate almond bark

Beat the peanut butter, butter and vanilla in a mixing bowl until blended. Add the confectioners' sugar and beat until smooth. Chill for 30 to 60 minutes. Shape the peanut butter mixture into balls.

Microwave the chocolate almond bark using package directions. Dip the peanut butter balls in the chocolate to coat. Arrange the balls on a sheet of waxed paper. Let stand until set.

Makes 4 to 5 dozen poppers

Holiday Rum Balls

1 1/2 cups vanilla wafer
    crumbs
1 cup confectioners' sugar

1 cup chopped pecans
3 tablespoons light corn
    syrup

1/4 teaspoon vanilla extract
Rum to taste
Confectioners' sugar

Combine the vanilla wafer crumbs, 1 cup confectioners' sugar, pecans, corn syrup and vanilla in a bowl and mix well. Add just enough rum to make a mixture that adheres.

Shape the crumb mixture into small balls and coat with additional confectioners' sugar. Store in an airtight container. May be prepared 1 to 2 weeks in advance.

Makes 1 1/2 to 2 dozen rum balls

* *

Amaretto Truffles

12 ounces semisweet
    chocolate
1/2 cup (1 stick) butter

2 egg yolks
1/2 cup whipping cream
1/4 cup amaretto

Finely chopped almonds or
    baking cocoa

Heat the chocolate in a double boiler over hot water until melted. Remove from heat. Add the butter 1 tablespoon at a time, stirring well after each addition.

Beat the egg yolks in a mixing bowl until pale yellow and thickened. Stir 1/4 cup of the hot chocolate mixture into the egg yolks. Stir the egg yolks into the hot mixture. Add the whipping cream and amaretto and mix well.

Cook for 1 minute or until the mixture is smooth and thickened, stirring constantly. Chill, covered, for 8 to 10 hours or until firm enough to shape into balls. Shape the chocolate mixture into balls. Coat with almonds or baking cocoa. Store in an airtight container in the refrigerator.

Makes 14 (2 1/2-inch) truffles or 42 (1-inch) truffles

Chocolate Spice Truffles

6 ounces gingersnap cookies

8 ounces bittersweet
    chocolate

2 tablespoons spiced rum

2 tablespoons strong coffee

1/2 cup (1 stick) unsalted
    butter

1/2 teaspoon cinnamon

1/2 teaspoon ginger

3 tablespoons confectioners'
    sugar, sifted

2 tablespoons baking cocoa,
    sifted

Process the cookies in a food processor until finely crushed. Heat the chocolate, spiced rum and coffee in a double boiler over hot water until blended, stirring frequently. Add the butter gradually, mixing well after each addition. Stir in the cookie crumbs, cinnamon and ginger. Cool slightly. Chill, covered, for 2 hours.

    Mix the confectioners' sugar and baking cocoa in a bowl. Shape the chilled dough by teaspoonfuls into 1-inch balls. Coat the balls with the confectioners' sugar mixture and place on a baking sheet. Chill, covered, until 1 hour before serving. Freeze for up to 1 month.

    Makes 3 dozen truffles

Contributed by Mimi Rippee

* * * * * * * * * * * * * * * * * * *

Easy Elegant Truffles

2 cups semisweet chocolate
    chips

1 teaspoon vanilla extract

1 teaspoon any natural
    extract or vanilla extract

3/4 cup sweetened
    condensed milk

1/8 teaspoon salt

Heat the chocolate chips in a double boiler over hot water until melted, stirring occasionally. Remove from heat. Stir in the flavorings, condensed milk and salt. Chill for 45 minutes or until the mixture is of a consistency that is easy to shape.

    Shape the chocolate mixture into 1-inch balls with buttered hands. Chill until firm. Coat with baking cocoa, flaked coconut, crushed nuts or confectioners' sugar.

    Makes 1 1/2 dozen truffles

Rocky Road Fudge Bars

FUDGE BARS

1/2 cup (1 stick)
   margarine
1 ounce unsweetened
   chocolate
1 cup sugar
1 cup flour
1 teaspoon baking
   powder
2 eggs, lightly beaten
1 teaspoon vanilla extract
1/2 to 1 cup chopped nuts

FOR THE BARS, heat the margarine and chocolate in a saucepan until blended, stirring frequently. Remove from heat. Stir in the sugar, flour, baking powder, eggs and vanilla. Fold in the nuts. Spread the batter in a greased and floured 9×13-inch baking pan.

FOR THE FILLING, combine the cream cheese, sugar, margarine, flour, egg and vanilla in a mixing bowl. Beat until smooth and fluffy, scraping the bowl occasionally. Stir in the nuts. Spread over the prepared layer. Sprinkle with the chocolate chips. Bake at 350 degrees for 30 to 35 minutes or until the edges pull from the sides of the pan. Sprinkle with the marshmallows. Bake for 2 minutes longer.

FOR THE TOPPING, combine the margarine, cream cheese and chocolate in a saucepan. Cook until blended, stirring frequently. Add the confectioners' sugar, milk and vanilla and mix until of a spreading consistency. Spread the topping over the hot layers. Let stand until cool. Cut into bars.

Makes 3 dozen bars

**CREAMY CHOCOLATE
FILLING**

6 ounces cream cheese,
   softened
1/2 cup sugar
1/4 cup (1/2 stick)
   margarine
2 tablespoons flour
1 egg
1/2 teaspoon vanilla
   extract
1/4 cup chopped nuts
1 cup chocolate chips
2 cups marshmallows

TOPPING

1/4 cup (1/2 stick)
   margarine
2 ounces cream cheese
1 ounce unsweetened
   chocolate
1 (1-pound) package
   confectioners' sugar
1/4 cup milk
1 teaspoon vanilla extract

Auntie's Brownies

1 1/2 ounces baking
   chocolate
1/2 cup (1 stick) butter
3/4 cup sugar

3/4 cup sifted flour
2 eggs, beaten
1 tablespoon vanilla extract

2/3 cup chopped walnuts or
   pecans
Confectioners' sugar

Heat the chocolate and butter in a saucepan until blended. Stir in the sugar, flour, eggs and vanilla. Add the walnuts and mix well. Spread the batter in a greased and floured 8×8-inch baking pan.

   Bake at 350 degrees for 15 to 18 minutes for super-moist brownies, or for 18 to 25 minutes for cakelike brownies. Cool in pan on a wire rack. Sprinkle with confectioners' sugar and cut into squares.

   Makes 1 1/3 to 2 dozen brownies

* *

Butter Pecan Turtle Bars

2 cups flour
1 cup packed light brown
   sugar
1/2 cup (1 stick) butter,
   softened

1 cup pecan halves
2/3 cup butter or margarine,
   melted

1/2 cup packed light brown
   sugar
1 cup milk chocolate chips

Beat the flour, 1 cup brown sugar and 1/2 cup butter in a mixing bowl until of a fine crumb consistency. Press the crumb mixture over the bottom of an ungreased 9×13-inch baking pan. Sprinkle with the pecans.

   Combine 2/3 cup melted butter and 1/2 cup brown sugar in a saucepan. Bring to a boil over medium heat, stirring constantly. Boil for 1 minute, stirring constantly. Drizzle over the pecans.

   Bake at 350 degrees for 18 to 20 minutes or until set. Sprinkle with the chocolate chips. Cool in pan on a wire rack. Cut into bars.

   Makes 3 dozen bars

Mimi's Biscotti

1/2 cup (1 stick) unsalted
  butter, softened
1 cup sugar
1 teaspoon baking powder
1/2 teaspoon baking soda

3 eggs, at room temperature
1 teaspoon vanilla extract
2 1/4 cups flour
1 cup chopped dried fruit

3/4 cup coarsely chopped
  almonds, hazelnuts,
  pecans or pistachios

Beat the butter in a mixing bowl until creamy. Add the sugar, baking powder and baking soda. Beat until light and fluffy. Beat in the eggs and vanilla until smooth. Add 2 cups of the flour and beat just until combined. Fold in the dried fruit and almonds with a wooden spoon. Chill, covered, for 4 to 10 hours.

Divide the dough into 2 equal portions. Place 1 portion of the dough on a hard work surface. Use a small amount of the remaining 1/4 cup flour to shape 1 portion of the dough into a log approximately 2 inches in diameter. Arrange the log along the long side of a baking sheet sprayed with nonstick cooking spray. Repeat the process with the remaining portion of dough. Pat each log into rectangle about 1/2 inch in height.

Place the logs immediately in a preheated 350-degree oven. Bake for 20 minutes or until light golden brown and slightly firm to the touch. Remove from oven. Cool the logs on the baking sheet on a wire rack for 10 minutes. Reduce the oven temperature to 250 degrees.

Place the logs on a cutting board using a metal spatula. Cut each log diagonally into 1/2-inch slices. Arrange the slices cut side down on a baking sheet. Dry in the oven for 30 minutes; turn. Dry for 30 minutes longer. Both sides should be hard and dry. If necessary reduce the oven temperature to 200 degrees and dry for 1 hour longer. Remove to a wire rack to cool completely. Store in sealable plastic bags. May freeze for up to 1 month. You may use dried cranberries, dried cherries, dried apricots, dried blueberries, dark or golden raisins as well as coconut for the chopped dried fruit.

Be creative. Try cherry almond, cranberry pistachio, golden raisin pecan, hazelnut apricot or your favorite combinations. You may also add cinnamon, poppy seeds, sweet citrus oil, citrus zest or any other extracts.

Makes 5 dozen biscotti

Contributed by Mimi Rippee

English Tea Cakes

CRUST

1 cup flour

1/2 cup (1 stick) butter, softened

1/4 cup packed brown sugar

FILLING

1 1/2 cups packed brown sugar

1/2 cup shredded coconut

2 tablespoons flour

2 eggs

1/2 teaspoon salt

1/2 teaspoon vanilla extract

FOR THE CRUST, beat the flour, butter and brown sugar in a mixing bowl until blended. Pat over the bottom and partially up the sides of an 8×11-inch baking pan. Bake at 350 degrees for 10 minutes.

FOR THE FILLING, beat the brown sugar, coconut, flour, eggs, salt and vanilla in a mixing bowl until combined. Spoon over the baked layer. Bake for 25 minutes. Cool in pan on a wire rack. Cut into squares or bars.

Makes 3 to 4 dozen squares

* *

Cherry Winks

2 1/4 cups flour

1 teaspoon baking powder

1/2 teaspoon baking soda

1 cup sugar

3/4 cup shortening

2 eggs

2 tablespoons milk

Vanilla extract to taste

1 cup chopped pecans

1 cup chopped dates

1/3 cup chopped maraschino cherries

2 1/2 cups cornflake crumbs or finely chopped nuts

Maraschino cherries, chopped

Mix the flour, baking powder and baking soda together. Beat the sugar and shortening in a mixing bowl until creamy. Add the eggs, milk and vanilla and beat until blended. Add the flour mixture and beat until smooth. Stir in the pecans, dates and 1/3 cup chopped maraschino cherries.

Drop the dough by teaspoonfuls into the cornflake crumbs and turn to coat. Arrange on a cookie sheet. Top each with a maraschino cherry piece. Bake at 350 degrees for 12 to 15 minutes or until light brown. Cool on cookie sheet for 2 minutes. Remove to a wire rack to cool completely.

Makes 2 to 3 dozen cookies

Gourmet Chocolate Chip Cookies

5 cups rolled oats

3 1/2 cups flour

2 teaspoons baking soda

1 teaspoon baking powder

2 teaspoons salt

1/2 teaspoon cinnamon

1 cup (2 sticks) butter, softened

2 cups sugar

2 cups packed brown sugar

4 eggs

2 teaspoons vanilla extract

4 cups chocolate chips

3 cups chopped nuts

8 ounces milk chocolate
candy bar, grated

Process the oats in a blender until of the consistency of a fine powder. Combine the ground oats, flour, baking soda, baking powder, salt and cinnamon in a bowl and mix well. Beat the butter and sugar in a mixing bowl until creamy. Add the eggs and vanilla and beat until smooth. Add the flour mixture gradually, beating constantly until blended. Stir in the chocolate chips, nuts and grated chocolate.

Drop the dough by rounded teaspoonfuls onto a cookie sheet. Bake at 375 degrees for 8 to 10 minutes or until light brown. Cool on cookie sheet for 2 minutes. Remove to a wire rack to cool completely. Store in an airtight container.

Makes 4 to 6 dozen cookies

* *

Mama's Oatmeal Cookies

1 cup shortening

1 cup packed brown sugar

3/4 cup sugar

2 eggs, beaten

2 teaspoons vanilla extract

1 teaspoon baking soda

1 teaspoon salt

1/4 teaspoon cinnamon

1 1/2 cups flour

3 cups rolled oats

1 cup chopped nuts

Beat the shortening, brown sugar and sugar in a mixing bowl until creamy. Add the eggs, vanilla, baking soda, salt and cinnamon and beat until blended. Add the flour, oats and nuts in the order listed, mixing well after each addition.

Shape the dough into 1-inch balls. Arrange on a greased cookie sheet and flatten slightly. Bake at 325 degrees for 10 to 12 minutes or until light brown. Cool on cookie sheet for 2 minutes. Remove the cookies to a sheet of waxed paper using a spatula. Cool for 1 hour before storing in an airtight container.

Makes 5 to 6 dozen

Cranberry Oatmeal Cookies

1 1/2 cups flour
1 teaspoon baking soda
1 teaspoon cinnamon
1/2 teaspoon salt
1 cup packed brown sugar

1/2 cup sugar
1 cup (2 sticks) margarine, softened
2 eggs
1 teaspoon vanilla extract

3 cups quick-cooking oats or rolled oats
1 (6-ounce) package craisins
1 cup chopped pecans

Mix the flour, baking soda, cinnamon and salt together. Beat the brown sugar, sugar and margarine in a mixing bowl until creamy. Add the eggs and vanilla and beat until smooth. Beat in the flour mixture. Stir in the oats, craisins and pecans.

Drop the dough by rounded teaspoonfuls onto an ungreased cookie sheet. Bake at 350 degrees for 9 to 10 minutes or until golden brown. Cool on cookie sheet for 1 minute. Remove to a wire rack to cool completely. To prepare for future use, drop the dough by teaspoonfuls onto a cookie sheet and freeze. Remove the frozen cookies to a sealable freezer bag and freeze until just before baking.

Makes 4 dozen cookies

* *

World's Best Sugar Cookies

5 cups flour
2 teaspoons baking soda
2 teaspoons cream of tartar
2 cups sugar

1 cup (2 sticks) butter or margarine, softened
1 cup vegetable oil
2 eggs

1 teaspoon vanilla extract
1/2 teaspoon salt
Sugar to taste

Sift the flour, baking soda and cream of tartar together. Beat 2 cups sugar and butter in a mixing bowl until creamy. Add the oil, eggs, vanilla and salt and beat until blended. Beat in the flour mixture.

Shape the dough into 1 1/2-inch balls. Coat with additional sugar. Place 2 inches apart on a cookie sheet. Flatten with a glass dipped in sugar. Bake at 350 degrees for 10 to 15 minutes or until light brown. Cool on cookie sheet for 2 minutes. Remove to a wire rack to cool completely. May shape the dough into logs, chill and slice as desired. Frost if desired, omitting the coating process.

Makes 4 to 5 dozen cookies

Walnut Toffee Chip Cookies

1 1/2 cups flour, sifted
1/2 teaspoon baking soda
1/2 teaspoon salt
1/2 cup (1 stick) butter, softened

1/2 cup packed brown sugar
1/3 cup sugar
1 egg
1 1/2 teaspoons vanilla extract

1/4 teaspoon water
1 cup mini semisweet chocolate chips
1 cup English toffee bits
1 cup chopped walnuts

Mix the flour, baking soda and salt together. Beat the butter, brown sugar and sugar in a mixing bowl at medium speed until light and fluffy. Add the egg, vanilla and water and beat until smooth. Add the flour mixture 1/2 cup at a time, beating constantly at low speed until a soft dough forms. Fold in the chocolate chips, toffee bits and walnuts.

Drop the dough by rounded teaspoonfuls 2 inches apart onto 2 ungreased cookie sheets. Bake at 375 degrees for 7 minutes or until golden brown. Cool on cookie sheets for 2 minutes. Remove to a wire rack to cool completely.

Makes 4 dozen cookies

* *

Banana Pie Supreme

2/3 cup sugar
6 tablespoons cake flour
1/4 teaspoon salt
1 3/4 cups milk
2 egg yolks, lightly beaten

1 1/4 teaspoons vanilla extract
1/2 cup whipping cream, whipped
3 bananas, sliced

1 baked (9-inch) pie shell
Juice of 1/2 lemon
Whipped cream
1 tablespoon grated orange zest

Combine the sugar, cake flour and salt in a double boiler and mix well. Stir in the milk. Cook over hot water until thickened, stirring constantly. Cook for 15 minutes longer, stirring occasionally.

Add a small amount of the hot custard to the egg yolks and mix well. Stir the egg yolk mixture into the hot custard mixture. Cook for 2 minutes, stirring constantly. Let stand until cool. Stir in the vanilla. Chill, covered, in the refrigerator. Fold in the whipped cream.

Layer the custard and bananas in the pie shell. Drizzle the lemon juice over the bananas. Garnish with additional whipped cream and sprinkle with the orange zest. Chill until serving time.

Serves 6 to 8

Fresh Berry Crumb Pie

CRUST

1 cup almonds

2 cups flour

1/2 cup sugar

3/4 cup (1 1/2 sticks) butter, chilled, cut into small pieces

BERRY FILLING

1/2 cup sugar

1 1/2 tablespoons cornstarch

2 pints fresh blueberries, raspberries and/or strawberries

FOR THE CRUST, spread the almonds in a single layer in a medium baking pan. Toast at 350 degrees for about 10 minutes or until light brown. Increase the oven temperature to 450 degrees. Process the almonds in a food processor for 10 seconds or until finely ground.

Combine the almonds, flour and sugar in a bowl and mix well. Cut in the butter with a pastry blender or 2 knives until crumbly. Press half the crumb mixture over the bottom and up the side of a 9-inch tart pan or pie plate.

FOR THE FILLING, combine the sugar and cornstarch in a bowl and mix well. Fold in the berries. Spoon the berry mixture into the prepared tart pan. Sprinkle with the remaining crumb mixture. Bake for 30 minutes or until brown and bubbly. Cool in pan on a wire rack.

Serves 6 to 8

* * * * * * * * * * * * * * * * * * * *

Having been settled in less than a day, portions of Oklahoma, including the Cherokee Strip, were nearly grown at birth. Not long after, a movement was started for Oklahoma to become a state. A major issue was whether Oklahoma Territory and Indian Territory should become two states or one.

On November 16, 1907, Oklahoma, with the Panhandle added, became a full-fledged state only fourteen years after the Cherokee Strip Land Run. A symbolic marriage was performed in Guthrie with an Indian girl and a young settler signifying a union of the two territories.

Black Bottom Pie

1 package chocolate
   sandwich cookies,
   crushed
6 tablespoons margarine,
   almost melted

16 ounces cream cheese,
   softened
3/4 cup confectioners'
   sugar

2 (4-ounce) packages French
   vanilla or white
   chocolate instant
   pudding mix
16 ounces whipped topping

Reserve 1/2 cup of the cookie crumbs. Combine the remaining cookie crumbs and margarine in a bowl and mix well. Press the crumb mixture over the bottoms and up the sides of two 8-inch pie plates. Freeze while preparing the filling. Beat the cream cheese and confectioners' sugar in a mixing bowl until creamy. Spread the cream cheese mixture in the prepared pie plates. Place in the freezer.

Prepare the pudding mixes using package directions. Spread over the prepared layers. Top with the whipped topping and sprinkle with the reserved cookie crumbs. Store, covered, in the refrigerator.

Makes 2 pies

* * * * * * * * * * * * * * * * * * * *

My Favorite Chocolate Pie

1 1/2 cups sugar
1/2 cup baking cocoa
1/3 cup cornstarch
1/8 teaspoon salt
2 cups milk

3 egg yolks, beaten
1 teaspoon vanilla extract
1 teaspoon butter or
   margarine
1 baked (9-inch) pie shell

3 egg whites
1/2 teaspoon vanilla extract
1/4 teaspoon cream of tartar
6 tablespoons sugar

Combine 1 1/2 cups sugar, baking cocoa, cornstarch and salt in a saucepan and mix well. Add the milk gradually, stirring constantly. Cook over medium heat until bubbly, stirring constantly. Cook for 2 minutes longer, stirring constantly. Remove from heat. Stir a large tablespoon of the hot mixture into the egg yolks. Stir the egg yolk mixture into the hot chocolate mixture. Cook for 2 minutes, stirring constantly. Remove from heat. Stir in 1 teaspoon vanilla and butter. Spoon into the pie shell.

Beat the egg whites, 1/2 teaspoon vanilla and cream of tartar in a mixing bowl until soft peaks form. Add 6 tablespoons sugar gradually, beating until stiff glossy peaks form. Spread over the prepared layer. Bake at 350 degrees for 12 to 15 minutes or until light brown. Let stand until cool.

Serves 6 to 8

Chocolate Chip Cookie Pie

2 eggs
1/2 cup flour
1/2 cup sugar
1/2 cup packed brown sugar

1/2 cup (1 stick) butter, softened
1 cup semisweet chocolate chips

1 cup pecans, chopped
1 unbaked (9-inch) pie shell

Beat the eggs in a mixing bowl at high speed for 3 minutes or until frothy. Add the flour, sugar and brown sugar and beat until blended. Beat in the butter. Stir in the chocolate chips and pecans.

Spoon the chocolate mixture into the pie shell. Bake at 325 degrees for 55 to 60 minutes or until the center is set. Let stand until cool.

Serves 8

* * * * * * * * * * * * * * * * * * * *

German Chocolate Pie

1 1/2 cups sugar
3 tablespoons baking cocoa
1/8 teaspoon salt
2 eggs, lightly beaten
3/4 cup evaporated milk

1/2 teaspoon vanilla extract
1 cup shredded coconut
1/4 cup (1/2 stick) butter, melted

1/2 cup (or more) chopped nuts
1 unbaked (9-inch) pie shell
Whipped cream

Combine the sugar, baking cocoa and salt in a bowl and mix well. Stir in the eggs. Add the evaporated milk and vanilla and mix well. Stir in the coconut, butter and nuts.

Spoon the chocolate filling into the pie shell. Bake at 350 degrees for 30 to 35 minutes or until set. Let stand until cool. Top each serving with a dollop of whipped cream.

Serves 6 to 8

Zesty Lemon Cream Pie

LEMON FILLING

1 cup sugar

5 tablespoons flour

1/4 teaspoon salt

1 cup water

1 cup evaporated milk

3 egg yolks, lightly beaten

Grated zest and juice of
    2 lemons

2 tablespoons butter

MERINGUE AND PIE

1/2 cup cold water

2 tablespoons sugar

1 tablespoon cornstarch

3 egg whites

1/4 cup sugar

1 baked (9-inch) pie shell

FOR THE FILLING, combine the sugar, flour and salt in a saucepan and mix well. Stir in the water and evaporated milk. Add the egg yolks and mix well. Cook until thickened, stirring constantly. Stir in the lemon zest and lemon juice. Add the butter and mix until blended. Cool while preparing the meringue.

FOR THE MERINGUE AND PIE, combine the cold water, 2 tablespoons sugar and cornstarch in a saucepan and mix well. Cook until thickened, stirring constantly. Let stand until cool. Beat the egg whites in a mixing bowl until soft peaks form. Add 1/4 cup sugar gradually, beating constantly until stiff peaks form. Stir in the cooled mixture.

Spoon the filling into the pie shell. Spread with the meringue, sealing to the edge. Bake at 325 degrees for 30 minutes or until light brown. Let stand until cool. May be prepared several hours before serving.

Serves 6 to 8

Pastry Perfection

Never use cake flour; it's too soft. Pastry or all-purpose flour is best. For lighter pastry, add a pinch of baking powder to flour before mixing. Lard or shortening gives a more tender crust than butter or margarine. The water MUST be iced before adding to the mixture. Too much water toughens the pastry crust. The less the dough is handled, the flakier the crust. Chill dough for 1/2 hour before rolling. Always roll dough on a cool surface. Pastry rises and bakes quicker in high heat.

Peanut Butter Brownie Pie

1 package brownie mix of choice
1 unbaked (9-inch) pie shell
8 ounces whipped topping

3/4 cup confectioners' sugar
1/2 cup creamy peanut butter

8 ounces whipped topping
1/2 cup chopped peanuts
1/2 cup shaved chocolate

Prepare the brownie mix. Bake the pie shell using package directions, spreading the brownie batter over the bottom of the pie shell 10 minutes before the end of the baking process. Let stand until cool.

Beat 8 ounces whipped topping, confectioners' sugar and peanut butter in a mixing bowl until light and fluffy. (Add more confectioners' sugar for a sweeter taste or less for more of a peanut butter taste.) Spoon the peanut butter filling into the pie shell. Chill, covered, for 30 to 60 minutes. Spread 8 ounces whipped topping over the prepared layer. Sprinkle with the peanuts and chocolate. Chill until serving time.

Serves 6 to 8

* * * * * * * * * * * * * * * * * * * *

Raving Raspberry Pie

1 cup sugar
1/3 cup flour
1 1/3 cups sour cream
2 eggs, lightly beaten
1 teaspoon vanilla extract

2 (12-ounce) packages frozen raspberries, thawed
1 unbaked (10-inch) deep-dish pie shell

1/3 cup flour
1/3 cup packed brown sugar
3 tablespoons butter, softened
1/3 cup chopped pecans

Combine the sugar and 1/3 cup flour in a bowl and mix well. Stir in the sour cream, eggs and vanilla. Fold in the raspberries. Spoon the raspberry mixture into the pie shell. Bake at 350 degrees for 45 to 50 minutes, shielding the crust with foil to prevent overbrowning 15 to 20 minutes before the end of the baking process if necessary.

Combine 1/3 cup flour, brown sugar and butter in a bowl and mix with a fork until crumbly. Stir in the pecans. Sprinkle the crumb mixture over the baked layer. Bake for 15 minutes longer.

Serves 8

Making Fruit Pie Fillings

Use this chart to make fillings for either double-crust or crumb-topped fruit pies. For the desired fruit filling, stir together the sugar and flour in a large mixing bowl. Add the fruit and toss until the fruit is coated with the sugar mixture. Continue as directed in recipe.

When making blackberry, blueberry, cherry, peach, raspberry, or rhubarb pies, you may also use frozen fruit. If using frozen fruit, toss it with the sugar-flour mixture, then let the mixture stand for 15 to 30 minutes or until the fruit is partially thawed but still icy. Stir well. Transfer to the pastry-lined pie plate. Top filling with pastry or crumb topping as directed in the recipe. Cover edge with foil. Bake for 50 minutes. Remove foil; bake for 20 to 30 minutes longer or until the top is golden brown and the fruit is tender.

Fruit	Amount of Fruit	Sugar	All-Purpose Flour
Apples, peeled, cored, and thinly sliced	6 cups	$1/2$ to $3/4$ cup	1 tablespoon
Apricots, pitted and sliced	4 cups	$1 1/4$ cups	$1/3$ cup
Blackberries	4 cups	$3/4$ to 1 cup	$1/4$ cup
Blueberries	4 cups	$1/2$ to $3/4$ cup	3 tablespoons
Cherries, tart red, pitted	4 cups	1 to $1 1/4$ cups	$1/4$ cup
Gooseberries, stemmed	4 cups	1 cup	$1/4$ cup
Nectarines, pitted and thinly sliced	6 cups	$1/2$ to $3/4$ cup	3 tablespoons
Peaches, peeled, pitted, and thinly sliced	6 cups	$1/2$ to $3/4$ cup	3 tablespoons
Pears, peeled, cored, and thinly sliced	6 cups	$1/3$ to $1/2$ cup	$1/4$ cup
Raspberries	5 cups	$1/2$ to $3/4$ cup	3 tablespoons
Rhubarb, cut into 1-inch pieces	4 cups	1 cup	$1/4$ cup

Contributors

Elizabeth Allen
Janet Allison
Alpha Respite Care Center
Kelly Anderson
Gwen Angilan
Mary Armstrong
Cheryl Arnold
Agnes Arvizu
Johnnie Atwood
Katy Atwood
Carolyn Bearden
Diana Beaulieu
Betty Behring
Paula Benge
Molly Biershaar
Alicia Martinez Bisel
Mrs. John Bowers
Artie Britt
Diane Brown
Ann Sears Bryant
Pat Burdick
Mary Butler
Kelly Callant
Kelli Cannon
Clara Chaffin
Christianne Garber Chase
Kris Atwood Cherry
Patricia Chesshir
Kimberly Coker
Jill Combrink
Chelsea Conrady
Bea Cooper
Kathi Youngblood Cooper
Ann and Richard Crump
Mim Cunningham
April Davis
Tary Davis
Florelee Day
Diabetes Center of
Oklahoma
Michelle Dick
Mika Dick
Annie Dillingham
Kay Dillingham
Sherrie Dinsmore
Teri Durr
Mabel Ebby
Susan Elliott
Packy Evans

Henrietta Fleshman
Bill Forster
Dina Fothergill
Diane Frantz
Sheliah Freeman
Nancy Fry
Ginny Geis
Kristin Gibson
Elsie Gillespie
Janice Gopfert
Sidney Gosnell
Grace Hale
Kathy Hannah
Jo Ann Harmon
Sue Harper
Armene Caroline Harris
Karey Henderson
Carol Henneman
Mrs. Marietta Henson
Joan Hibbits
Dorothy Hladik
Shawn Groendyke Hodgen
Tandi Hoelker
Christi Holland
Raymie Holland
Jill Holthoff
Thelma Horrall
Pam Hunt-Rolen
Mary Helen Iselin
Lora Jacks
Nancy Jeronimus
Cathie Jones
Sherrel Jones
Marolyn Jump
Frances Kehnemund
Mary Kay Kennedy
Ann Killian
Jennifer Kisling
Mrs. Sandy Kitterman
Suzanne Klemme
Pam Koehn
Matt Krodel
La Luna Blu Restaurant
Kay Lamerton
Eilena Laubhan
Rosalie Lawrence
John and Mona Loewen
Ellen Lohrenz
Jeannine Long

May Doris Longley
Marie H. Luke
Melody Manahan
Maple Place Bed and
Breakfast
Barbara Marquis
Cheryl Martens
Virgie Martens
Carol Mayer
Alice McCarley
Mrs. Ben. P. McCarley
Jill McCarley
Suzanne McCreary
Claire McLinn
Lori McMillin
Lora F. Meier
Sharon Melrose
Celia Merritt
Cyndy Meyer
Mrs. Louise Milacek
Jocelyn Miller
Mary Miller
Rosemary Moore
Lori Morrison
Kathy Mulholland
Carolyn Nicholas
Ila Nicholas
Jo Ann Nicholas
Molly Nicholas
Sue Ann Norrie
Judy O'Connell
Kelley E. Olson
Barbar O'Quin
Effie Hronopulos Outhier
Linda Outhier
Marty Oyler
Rebecca Redding Parry
Barbara Patterson
Kristy Pendleton
Sharon L. Phares
Jill Phillips
Mary Beth Phillips
Molly Player
Jane Pond
Jane Rainey
Mrs. Lilly Rascoe
Nelda Ream
Janice Reed
Josie Riddick

Mimi Rippee
Gail Roberts
Kristi Roberts
Faith Sarver
Verna Schaefer
Pam Schoenhals
Marcia Seals
Debra Sexton
Mary Lynn Shamblin
Maxine Shepard
Belva Shimanek
Evelyn Shimanek
Tracy Shimanek
Sally Shipley
Janice Smith
Jo Smith
Valorie Smith
Jo Spotts
Ebby Stratton
Tana Stufflebean
Wilma Stufflebean
Elvada Sullivan
Mashell Swenn
Eva Taylor
Janie Timmermeier
Rick Tozzi
Sharon Trojan
Jo Tucker
Sue Unruh
Beverly J. Voth
Shannon Waken
Mrs. Jan Walton
Leslie Weldon
Sally Whiteneck
Linda Barton Wiens
Gabriella Wilson
Reneé Winter Winklejohn
Katrena Winter
Sue Frizell Winter
Sherry Wolff
Helen Wood
Janie Word
Cindy Worthington
Charlotte Wycoff
Gail Wynne
Phillip and Toni Yancer
Sarah Yauk
Billye Jean Zimmer

Index

Chicken Kabobs, 92
Chicken Ro-Tel, 94
Chicken Tetrazzini, 98
Crab-Stuffed Mushrooms, 28
Crustless Quiche, 127
Fresh Green Beans in a
    Pouch, 108
Mexican Chicken and Rice
    Casserole, 98
Mixed Green Salad with
    Warm Portobello Balsamic
    Vinaigrette, 60
Seafood with White Wine
    Sauce, 101
Spinach Quiche, 126
Stuffed Flank Steak, 77
Stuffed Mushrooms, 29
Tarragon Chicken, 96
Warm Portobello Balsamic
    Vinaigrette, 60
Wild Rice and Mushroom
    Soup, 48
Wyoming Chili, 43

Pasta. *See also* Sauces, Pasta
Awesome Spaghetti, 87
Cavitini, 80
Chicken Ro-Tel, 94
Chicken Tetrazzini, 98
Cool Cucumber Salad, 63
Fettuccini Alfredo, 115
Linguini alla Puttanesca, 116
Luncheon Chicken
    Salad, 66
Penne with Artichokes, 116
Pork and Pasta with Bacon
    Balsamic Vinaigrette, 86

Shirley Bellmon's Homemade
    Chicken and Noodles, 91
Sweet-and-Sour Macaroni
    Salad, 63

Pastry, 153
Sugar Cookie Crust, 152
Wheat Germ Crust, 125

Peanut Butter
Peanut Butter Brownie Pie, 182
Peanut Butter Cake, 161
Peanut Butter
    Frosting, 161
Peanut Butter Poppers, 168

Pies
Banana Pie Supreme, 177
Black Bottom Pie, 179
Chocolate Chip Cookie
    Pie, 180
Fresh Berry Crumb Pie, 178
German Chocolate Pie, 180
My Favorite Chocolate Pie, 179
Peanut Butter Brownie Pie, 182
Raving Raspberry Pie, 182
Zesty Lemon Cream Pie, 181

Pineapple
Chicken Kabobs, 92
Fresh Cranberry Relish, 54
Jamaican Jungle Bread, 133
Marshmallow Dip with Fresh
    Fruit Kabobs, 19
Pineapple Dressing, 66
Pineapple Sheet Cake, 162
Watergate Salad, 55

Pork. *See also* Ham; Sausage
Pork and Pasta with Bacon
    Balsamic Vinaigrette, 86
Pork Tenderloin with Spicy
    Mustard Sauce, 85
Pork with Green Chiles, 87

Potatoes
Dill Potatoes, 112
Fantastic Potato Salad, 61
French Red Potato Salad
    with Balsamic Herb
    Dressing, 62
Low-Fat Potato Soup, 47
Make-Ahead Mashed
    Potatoes, 112
Quick Clean-Up Chicken, 92
Roasted Vegetables, 78
Stuffed Baked Potatoes, 113

Poultry. *See* Chicken; Turkey

Puddings
Southern Bread
    Pudding, 148
Ultimate Banana
    Pudding, 149

Pumpkin
Autumn Pumpkin Soup, 48
Pumpkin Bread, 134

Quiches
Crustless Quiche, 127
Spinach Quiche, 126
Wheat Germ Onion
    Quiche, 125

Raspberry
Creamy Gelatin Surprise, 149
Raspberry Almond Tart, 153
Raspberry Muffins, 137
Raving Raspberry Pie, 182

Rice
Chinese Fried Rice, 119
Green Chile Rice, 119
Jambalaya, 46
Mexican Chicken and Rice
Casserole, 98
Wild Rice, 120
Wild Rice and Mushroom
Soup, 48
Wild Rice Salad, 64

Rolls
Cinnamon Rolls, 140
Mom's Homemade Hot Rolls, 141
Oatmeal Dinner Rolls, 141
Orange Crunchy Rolls, 131

Salad Dressings, 55, 59, 63
Balsamic Herb Dressing, 62
Banana Poppy Seed
Dressing, 68
Everyday Vinaigrette, 66
Herb Vinegar, 100
Lemon Vinaigrette, 100
Lime Vinaigrette, 65
Mustard Dressing, 58
Onion Dressing, 58
Pineapple Dressing, 66
Red Wine Dressing, 57
Roasted Garlic Dressing, 68
Sesame Poppy Dressing, 54
Simple Coleslaw
Dressing, 67
Soy Dressing, 64
Sweet-and-Sour Dressing, 63
Warm Portobello Balsamic
Vinaigrette, 60

Salads, Chicken
Chicken and Black Bean
Salad, 65
Luncheon Chicken
Salad, 66
Mango Chutney Chicken
Salad, 64

Salads, Fruit
Fresh Cranberry Relish, 54
Strawberry and Spinach
Salad, 54
Tossed Avocado Salad, 56
Watergate Salad, 55

Salads, Grain
Wild Rice Salad, 64

Salads, Pasta
Cool Cucumber Salad, 63
Luncheon Chicken
Salad, 66
Sweet-and-Sour Macaroni
Salad, 63

Salads, Potato
Fantastic Potato Salad, 61
French Red Potato Salad
with Balsamic Herb
Dressing, 62

Salads, Seafood
Shrimp Salad, 67

Salads, Vegetable
Antipasto Salad with
Vinaigrette Dressing, 55
Broccoli Raisin Salad, 56
Cabbage and Onion Slaw, 58
Caesar Salad à la
Tozzi, 57
Crunchy Tossed Salad, 57
Fiesta Corn Bread Salad, 59
Jackson Salad, 58
Mixed Green Salad with
Warm Portobello Balsamic
Vinaigrette, 60
Oriental Salad, 59
Strawberry and Spinach
Salad, 54

Salmon
Olive-Crusted Salmon with
Lemon Vinaigrette, 100
Pistachio Smoked Salmon
Spread, 22
Smoked Salmon, 30

Salsa
Aspen Salsa, 12
Black Bean Salsa, 13
Chunky Artichoke Salsa with
Pita Chips, 12
Corn Salsa, 13
Mango Salsa, 14

Sandwiches
Cucumber Sandwiches, 25
Southwest Sandwiches, 99

Sauces. *See also* Glazes;
Marinades
Mustard Sauce, 72

Oklahoma Barbecue Sauce, 104
Spicy Gravy, 76
Spicy Mustard Sauce, 85
Tarragon Sauce, 30
Whiskey Peppercorn
Sauce, 103

Sauces, Dessert
Butter Cream Sauce, 148
Praline Sauce, 148
Vanilla Cream Sauce, 154
Vanilla Sauce, 163
Warm Caramel Sauce, 158

Enid's Hometown Market

Serving Enid Since 1906
Farm Fresh Produce
Quality Select Meats
Low Prices Everyday
3 Convenient Locations

95th Year

THE BOYS MARKET

www.Enid Homes.com
Real Estate Listings - Coupons - Community Events - Recipes

Junior Welfare League of Enid
P.O. Box 5877
Enid, Oklahoma 73702

Name
_____

Street Address
_____

City _____   State _____   Zip _____

Telephone
_____

Your Order	Quantity	Total
Cooking by the BootStraps at $21.95 per book		$
Stir-Ups at $16.95 per book		$
Oklahoma residents add 8.35% sales tax		$
Shipping and handling at $3.05 per book		$
Total		$

Method of Payment: [   ] MasterCard   [   ] VISA
                     [   ] Check payable to Junior Welfare League of Enid

Account Number _____   Expiration Date _____

Cardholder Name
_____

Signature
_____

Photocopies accepted